LEGENDARY WIDOWS

STORIES OF LEGACY

Carolyn Moor

MODERN WIDOWS CLUB

ABOUT MODERN WIDOWS CLUB

Modern Widows Club envisions a world in which every widow is valued as a human being and is seen as a vital part of their family, their work, and their community. Simply put, we provide compassionate support to widows, empowering them to thrive as they move from grief to growth.

We are, at our core, a women's health organization focused on worldwide widow well-being. We approach this profound emotional mission through lived experience and by creating solutions addressing problems due to imbalanced social systems. Our effective management and significant impact grows larger each year, empowering well-positioned widow leaders to accelerate progress every step of the way. We tackle complex challenges with sustained effort over many years while addressing consequences of the pandemic. Founded in 2011, we became a nonprofit organization in 2014, beginning as a widow-to-widow support system and evolving organically into widow mentoring and leadership, including our current active participation in advocacy movements.

From our recent comparable research data surveying 802 widows, findings confirm that Modern Widows Club provides programs to DECREASE the negative social determinants of health factors such as loneliness, depression, hopelessness, anger, sleep deprivation, and feeling overwhelmed while INCREASING and empowering more positive outcomes such as happiness, confidence, positive self image, sense of purpose, stronger interest in personal mental and physical self-care and emotional health, the promise of the future, and in interacting with others.

These results coincide with the well-researched data between the need for more "attachment solutions" to "detachment problems" in the mental health industry. Being traumatically, emotionally, mentally, and physically detached, such as in widowhood, causes both catalytic vulnerability and intensity in survivorship missions, requiring active response to acute needs.

Building trust, developing a sense of belonging, and creating opportunity for all widows is vital to delivering compassionate support within our many programs. Through our in-person communities, virtual communities (including those for Spanish speakers and widow survivors of suicide), empowerment events, e-courses, educational health webinars, social clubs (Book, Art, Travel, Dating and Parenting), we identify the challenges that are unique to widowhood and stand strong in the gap, pioneering widow support, solutions, and research.

844-4-A WIDOW
support@modernwidowsclub.org
https://modernwidowsclub.org
https://courses.modernwidowsclub.org

FOREWORD

Hello and welcome to this beautiful book, *Legendary Widows: Stories of Legacy*, honoring accomplished and renowned widows who have had a profound influence on me and millions of widows around the world, all of us searching for inspiration and light. I'm Carolyn Moor, founder and CEO of Modern Widows Club.

Whether you know a widow or are a widow yourself, you will deeply feel these stories, which will leave you, as they left me, with the belief that widowhood is a stage of life in which to blossom. You'll learn how leaning into widowhood—seeing it as a catalyst for extraordinary personal growth—brings great hope that continues long after loss. Indeed, you'll discover that widowed women are creators and sustainers of culture worldwide and that across the span of human history, widowed women have made immeasurable societal contributions.

Yet with over seventy percent of married women eventually entering widowhood—a steadily growing sector of our worldwide female population, increasing from one percent of women at age forty to seventy-three percent of women at age eighty-five—a significant number of their voices have never been heard, their lives made invisible. A project like this is born with the hope of compensating for this lack of exposure, created with the goal of reintroducing the world to these widowed women, spotlighting who they were, how they've lived, and what they've accomplished. This book is a clarion call to the world that widows matter, that their voices and lives touch every family on earth.

The brave, beautiful women whose experiences fill these pages honored the love they received, and in so doing allowed it to transform their stories, to strengthen and renew themselves as rays of light, waymakers, pioneers, trailblazers, compassionate leaders, honorable philanthropists, vow keepers, and pillars of womanhood.

From the beginning, when I first conceived creating a book that would represent the essence of the Modern Widows Club vision and mission, I knew that all the proceeds of the project would go toward serving and raising awareness for widows around the world. They need this. They deserve this. Revolutionizing the future of widowhood is the only path forward for millions anxiously awaiting its arrival. To get there, we need to shine a bright light on widow role models, showcasing their strength, inspiration, reinvention, influence, faith and courage.

As the founder of Modern Widows Club, nonprofit widow mentoring, leadership, and advocacy have been my life's work. I've spent two decades listening to tens of thousands of widows of every ethnicity, of all ages, of all backgrounds and circumstances, and have been blessed to be intimately included in their sacred spaces of healing, where widows tend to speak their own unique language of loss, love, and legacy.

While walking my own widowhood journey, and walking alongside other widows on theirs, I've heard their dreams and seen their pain quite clearly. With those powerful emotions in mind, I've nurtured Modern Widows Club from the grassroots of my living room to the global movement it is today, impacting widows as far afield as Israel, Africa, India, the Philippines, and the United Kingdom.

FOREWORD

At this point in my journey, I consider myself to be something of a subject matter expert. To that end, my vision and hope for all widows is that they may live in a world where every widow is valued and seen as a vital part of their family, of their work, and of their community because they remain, even and especially in their widowhood, extraordinary women who need empathy and compassionate support as they move from grief to growth. We cannot afford to miss this opportunity to change history for generations to come. Widows play an important role in healing the world. You will see this in every story in this book.

You'll notice that in each chapter every legendary widow's life trajectory is featured in three parts, her empowering story told over an arc of time—childhood life, married life, and widowhood life—each story sharing her visions, influences, worldly impacts, and life accomplishments. At the end of each chapter, I've included a section titled *Moor Thoughts*, in which I share my own heartfelt thoughts about why I specifically chose this particular brilliant woman, this extraordinary widow, who, as a shining light, directed and motivated me to shine my own light, who inspired my own legacy building process.

But why *Legendary Widows*? There's an interesting story, which fell into my lap. On September 9, 2021, I was cruising along on Twitter and decided to post a tweet about Terri Irwin. I'd often thought about how legendary her story had been while watching from afar over many years while on my own widowhood journey. I was inspired by the way she continued to honor her late husband Steve's memory and vision.

So, in this post, I serendipitously and fortuitously included the hashtag #legendarywidow. But then the strangest message popped up: *None found*. My mouth fell open. I'd never seen that message in all my years of social media, and as you no doubt know, it's quite hard indeed to find a hashtag that hasn't been used somewhere in the digital universe.

Right away I knew I'd discovered a surprising secret—no one had yet to team the word "legendary" with the word "widow"—

and was immediately moved to share the real truth about widows as role models and inspirational figures.

I began adding a "Legendary Widow" selection to every month's topic at Modern Widows Club. And since then, every year, we've given a Legendary Award to one special person who is heroic by virtue of the exemplary way they serve widows worldwide. Simply put, Legendary Widows create new ways of honoring what needs to be brought into the light.

As other widows began finding hope and light, they would discover their own inspirational widows and share them with me. My list began to grow with time, so much so that I now consider *Stories of Legacy* to be the first book in what will become the *Legendary Widows* series: *Stories of Strength; Stories of Courage; Stories of Resilience; Stories of Inspiration; Stories of Reinvention;* and *Stories of Faith.*

What I know for sure is that the world is filled with trailblazing, legendary widows. My hope is that you enjoy each story in the book and find these incredible journeys of womanhood and widowhood to be audacious celebrations of life. I certainly do.

Carolyn Moor, June 2023

INTRODUCTION

I'm Paul Chavez, one of the eight children of Helen Fabela Chavez and president of the Cesar Chavez Foundation, which keeps alive the legacy of my father. It is a privilege to prepare this introduction for Carolyn Moor's wonderful book about a group of courageous widows who served as pioneers and inspirations in their own rights. Ms. Moor places the adjective *legendary* before widow to show how these remarkable women served as genuine examples for all to emulate today and in future generations. Let me share a few stories showing why it is fitting that our mother is included in this book.

After she passed away in 2016, some well-meaning people described Helen Chavez using the often-repeated sentiment that behind every great man is a great woman. My brothers and sisters and I took exception to that notion. She never stood behind my dad—she stood by his side, and sometimes even out in front.

From when they married in 1948, my father would come home relating a fresh injustice in the fields and tell my mom, "Somebody's got to do something." After listening to my dad's continuing outrage over the farm workers' plight, my mother began telling him, "Why don't *you* do it."

Like most from their generation—and others—my parents and their siblings escaped farm labor. My father worked organizing the Community Service Organization (CSO), the largest and most effective Latino civil rights group in California during the 1950s and early '60s. My folks no longer had to scrimp to buy food or pay rent. They had a paid, week-long annual vacation. They built a middle-class life in East Los Angeles. But my dad couldn't live with himself without at least trying to help the farm workers whose lives he and my mother had shared. It wasn't just his dream; it was a shared dream.

In 1962, my mom and dad together made the fateful decision to give up their comfortable lifestyle, move back to the dusty, small Central Valley farm town of Delano, and return to the fields.

My father and mother knew there would be no paycheck and much sacrifice. My mother would have to go back to laboring in the fields with a young family of eight children to feed and to buy gas so my father could drive up and down the mammoth valley organizing farm workers. My mom recalled that first my dad asked her if she would give her consent, and would she help him in whatever she could do? She said, "Yes, I'll help you in whatever way I can." We had nothing to begin with anyways, my mother added, so what do we have to lose?

Sometimes in the early days, my dad returned home disheartened after spending days on the road without enlisting anyone. With no income and a wife and big family to support, he didn't know whether he would succeed and wondered whether he had done the right thing by putting his family through all this hardship. In his journal, he wrote: "It's hard. I don't know how much more I can put my family through." After my mother bucked him up, his next journal entry read, "Spoke to Helen today. I'm ready to continue."

With others, they went about methodically building the union they had dreamed about. Everything changed in 1965, when Filipino farm workers struck grape growers in the Delano,

California area. Growers historically pitted the races against each other—for example, by using Latinos to break Filipinos' strikes and vice versa. Everyone knew the history.

The Filipino grape strikers asked my dad's mostly Latino union to join their picket lines. My father's fledgling union debated whether to unite with the Filipinos on strike. My dad and the other early organizers had a long-term plan: Spend years organizing before resorting to major field walkouts. My mom was a person of few words, but when she did speak, she cut to the heart of things. "Are we a union or not?" Helen Chavez asked. That ended the debate. They joined the strike and the two unions merged the next year to form the United Farm Workers.

Throughout my father's career, my mom followed him wherever he went. They traveled around a lot during the '50s before moving to Delano in 1962, to begin creating the union. In 1971, my dad asked my mother to move with him to the new headquarters in the Tehachapi Mountain town of Keene, east of Bakersfield. It offered room to grow as the movement went national and a place where farm workers could come to be trained in how to run their own union.

This time, my mom refused to accompany him. The 187-acre site had been a county-run tuberculosis sanitarium in the 1930s and was where my mother was interned and mistreated. They decided my mom would be driven with the kids from Delano to Keene on weekends to visit my father.

Looking forward to seeing my dad, one weekend she arrived to find him gone. She learned this was one of the times federal agents notified the union of plots on his life. My father spent a few weeks on the road not sleeping in the same place twice. Finally, he told my mom, I'm not a coward. I haven't done anything wrong, except fight for workers' rights. I'm going back to work. If they kill me, then so be it, if that's God's will.

My mother said she told herself, Helen, you're being selfish. She remembered her vow of promising to be his partner. And here, he was risking his life to do what he thought was right. My mom moved us to Keene before Christmas 1971. Over time she came to love the place, but at first she put her own fears and bad memories aside because she had made a promise to help our father.

Our mother outlived our dad by 23 years, but she kept fulfilling the promises she had made to him and the movement. My mom was unfailingly humble and modest, and she avoided the limelight like there wasn't a tomorrow. She never spoke in public or was interviewed by reporters. But she would overcome her humility and speak up when it mattered.

One time it happened was when President Obama visited our Keene headquarters in 2012, to dedicate, in front of 7,000 people, the Cesar E. Chavez National Monument, the 398th unit of the National Park Service and the first recognizing a contemporary Latino figure. With our mother on his arm, the president laid a single red rose on his gravesite in the beautifully landscaped Memorial Garden. As they were walking away, we watched while she and the president paused. They were clearly talking about something. Later, we asked her what it was about.

My mom asked the president whether he would promise to do something about immigration reform. He replied, yes, Mrs. Chavez, I promise I will. This genuinely humble and shy woman was buttonholing the president of the United States to make a point.

In her quiet, gentle, and yet fiercely determined ways, our mom was an advocate and activist in her own right until her final days. She stood independently by, and sometimes out in front, of her husband. She shared those qualities with many of the other legendary widows chronicled in this book.

Paul F. Chavez
President, Cesar Chavez Foundation and Helen Fabela Chavez Estate
https://chavezfoundation.org

For Modern Widows Everywhere

Copyright © 2023 by MODERN WIDOWS CLUB

All rights reserved.

Wister is a registered trademark of Modern Widows Club, Inc. in the United States and/or other countries.

No part of this book may be reproduced in any form or by any electronic or mechanical means, including information storage and retrieval systems, without written permission from the author, except for the use of brief quotations in a book review.

1

HELEN FABELA CHAVEZ

Fierce Determination to Help Change Lives

Helen Fabela Chavez, widow of Cesar Chavez, picketed alongside her husband during the farm labor movement in the United States, got arrested in strikes in support of those laborers, and throughout this tumultuous time in their lives and the lives of millions of farm workers, somehow found the presence of mind and strength of character to raise the couple's eight children. Her family, said Cesar Chavez, could not have led the farmworkers' labor movement without Helen's support.

Born on January 21, 1928, in Brawley, California, Helen Fabela grew up in a converted barn near the Central Valley town of McFarland, California, and in nearby Delano, where she dropped out of high school to support her family by working in the fields. It was in Delano in the mid-1940s where she met her future husband, Cesar Chavez, while they were both laboring in the fields as farm workers. They corresponded while he served in the Navy and married upon his discharge in 1948.

After they were married, Cesar went back to work, toiling in the fields. He returned home to Helen after experiencing a new and deep injustice in the workplace. "Somebody's got to do something about it," he told her.

Helen understood the importance of the mission and nurtured her husband's dream of organizing farm workers. In 1962, she and their eight young children left behind a middle-class lifestyle and embraced voluntary poverty in support of her husband's labors.

During the early years of his mission, when Cesar would return home after a long stretch on the road, feeling alone and demoralized, not having recruited anyone into his new union, Helen would be his rock. She reminded him of the importance of his calling, encouraging him to keep working, to keep going. "Cesar, you have to have faith in God that what you're doing is right," she said.

The Chavez family moved often in the 1950s as Cesar organized the most effective Latino civil rights group of that era. In 1962, Cesar resigned from that job and moved to Delano to begin building what became the United Farm Workers (UFW). Helen went back to work in the fields to help their family survive while her husband traveled the California Central Valley recruiting farm workers for the union. She earned five dollars a week plus food and housing.

Helen worked in the background of the labor movement that rose to prominence in the 1960s and 1970s. Cesar led and helped establish the United Farm Workers of America, a union of poor immigrants—predominantly Mexican and Filipino—who worked the fields in the United States West and Southwest for little pay and under very poor working conditions. Under Cesar's strong leadership through strategically organized strikes in the Southwest, wages and working conditions gradually improved.

In 1965, during the Delano Grape Strike, Helen took the lead in managing the Farm Workers Credit Union, working full time at their office while maintaining a home life. She would often walk vineyard picket lines before dawn, then direct the business of the Credit Union, which she ran for more than twenty years before retiring. Under her direction, the Farm Workers Credit Union loaned more than $20 million to impoverished farm worker members and their families.

Her commitment to family was unflinching. In addition to raising her own children, Helen was a surrogate mother to many young volunteers who came to Delano and later to La Paz, UFW headquarters in Keene, California, to work with the movement.

Cesar died in 1993. With a few noted and life-affirming exceptions, Helen stayed out of the public eye for most of her remaining years. On her husband's behalf, a year after his death, she accepted the Medal of Freedom, the highest American honor for civilians, from United States President Bill Clinton. In 2003, upon the release of a United States commemorative stamp featuring her husband, she sat for a rare interview. In 2012, she met with United States President Barack Obama in Keene, the location of the Cesar Chavez Foundation, at a dedication for a national monument honoring Cesar's profound contributions to the nation's working class.

Upon her death in 2016 at age eighty-eight, her family released a statement saying Cesar Chavez would not have led the farmworker's labor movement if not for his wife's support.

Helen Chavez was quiet and humble but fiercely determined and strong-willed in the face of unrelenting obstacles and steep odds. She held deep convictions and acted on them. Her roles as an administrator, laborer, activist, wife, widow, and mother make her a role model for young girls and women to this day.

MOOR THOUGHTS ABOUT HELEN FABELA CHAVEZ

I was drawn to Helen because of her fierceness and strength and faith throughout the story of her helping build equity for farm laborers. The boldness and determination she and her husband brought toward fair labor, which was not welcomed by society at large, gave me a boost of courage to continue lifting up my own voice despite any pushback I may experience for supporting an unpopular cause.

Greatness isn't always a straight line. No one knew this more than Cesar and Helen in their brave pursuit of fair labor laws and policies both statewide and nationally. I admired and still admire their fight for injustices that were desperately, humanely needed for Latino men, women, and children who worked then —and work now—in farm labor. Helen struggled every day, fighting hard, earning every inch of respect for herself, her children, and for her people. She embodied the movement and became its inspirational face of determination.

What I learned from Helen and applied to the challenges of my own journey was that nothing along your path can replace the genuine sweat-equity experience when it comes to believing in and fighting for a cause. She knew she was the subject-matter expert from her long hours of working in the fields beside her family, day in and day out. She woke early to picket, then headed to the fields for long grueling days of backbreaking labor. Her indomitable spirit was an inspiration to generations of Latina women, yes, but also to women everywhere. To me. Her brilliant light and honorable heart inspire me even as I write this.

I picture her working in the fields or at the office while imagining a new and better future for each person laboring beside her, planning how best to take the next step to raise awareness and bring about necessary change. The cause and movement were personal to her, impacting the lives and livelihoods of her friends and family, activating her profound and effective mothering waypower.

The grit it takes to press on in the face of such overwhelming adversity, with all forces of power aligned against you, can only come from an internal place of divinity, of pure light of purpose. Helen tapped into this light within her and discovered her God-given right to fight for what was humanely equitable. A strength from above as well as within. If I could have met her, I imagine the light in her eyes would have been blazing bright.

I imagine that after Cesar's death, Helen must have channeled his essence, quietly chatting with him, in her mind, under her breath, like so many widows do, like I do with my late husband when I need to be consoled and guided. I find that to be one way through widowhood, an internal tactic to help face that grief and loss. For Helen, like for all of us, Cesar's physical body was gone, but not his love and not his mission, which remained ever so alive. His love, *their* love, was her fuel to keep living, to keep fighting, to move forward in ways that mattered to both of them. She picked up his torch, *their* torch, and never let it go out. Again, even now, I am filled with admiration for her.

A woman of conviction is a woman to reckon with. Helen was a quiet giant, my favorite kind of legendary woman. She was stern, strategic, poised, purposeful, driven, and loyal. Her life's purpose was to walk alongside her husband and share his cause. In the beginning, she did this by supporting him and their family but later, after his death, she had to walk their path alone. She was no stranger to survivor missions and became a role model for those who had to fight through that lonely battle, a role model for generations of Latinas, but also for all women who strive to live lives of high virtue and fierce determination—through marriage and widowhood.

I hope you will allow yourself to create and believe in a vision for your pathway forward. Helen created a new future for herself, hard won and toiled for, yes, but deeply fulfilling. I hope you will allow yourself to be inspired by her life story, by her owning her part in the movement of change, by lighting a fire for good in the world, and, in the process, by defining the kind of woman she was proud to become. Be encouraged. Allow your soul to fuel the light within you. Fan it diligently with your dreams, hopes, and courage like Helen did. That's what I do. And always will.

QUESTIONS TO CONSIDER

Helen believed in her husband's vision to promote equity for farm laborers and advance rights for himself and others facing the same challenges. Do you encourage others to believe in their dreams? Who do you inspire?

Humbleness is a virtue. Where does humbleness help you in your widowhood journey?

Has a faith in God (religious/spiritual) helped you through widowhood?

2

TERRI IRWIN

A Heart for Wildlife

Theresa "Terri" Raines Irwin is a born naturalist and animal lover, part of a family whose passion for the outdoors guides their work and their time together away from work.

Her father, Clarence Raines, frequently interrupted his driving while on his long-haul truck route from Eugene, Oregon, to rescue and bring home injured wildlife. From adorable Merganser ducklings to starving, nearly wild dogs and everything in between, long, cold nights would be deadly for injured animals, and Terri's father couldn't and wouldn't let the animals succumb to that fate. Once they were safe at the Raineses' house, Terri learned to care for these animals and then release them.

Her two older sisters were married and gone, leaving Terri to grow up as a kind of only child. She's described her early years as being a free-range kid, roaming the woods with friends, looking for rattlesnakes and other creatures—and learning how to care for them.

With her heart focused on wildlife, she trained as a veterinary assistant, purchased her first house at age eighteen, took the reins of the family trucking company at age twenty, and at the age of twenty-two, in 1988, started her own business.

Startled by a newspaper ad offering cougars for sale, she created a small rescue park, Cougar Country, to rescue captive and injured cougars, bobcats, bears, foxes, and raccoons. Her stated goal was to nurse them back to health and then release them into the wild. She also rescued birds, dogs, and other domesticated animals. She had so many dogs and cats, in fact, that when she began to help organize and set up children's zoos in local parks, she often used her own pets. It was hard work finding the balance between releasing those that were healthy enough and providing a home for those that had no other choice. Hard work and long hours. She was happy and fulfilled.

But in her 2007 book *Steve and Me*, she shared how important she'd felt it was to experience life and the world. And with that thought in mind in 1991, she agreed to take a trip to Australia with a friend.

It was there that the twenty-seven-year-old Terri met Steve Irwin, a larger-than-life animal lover who worked at his own family's rescue center. They were married within a year. Terri has written two books about their time together—*My Steve* and *Steve and Me*.

Their shared love for animals and their childhoods spent in the company of wildlife inspired their grand plans from the very beginning. His parents had brought him up to save persecuted wild and dangerous animals at what was then known as Beerwah Reptile Park in Queensland, Australia. She had been doing the very same thing at her father's house. They'd been living almost parallel lives.

Terri joined Steve in Australia, adding her years of animal experience in the United States to his years of experience in the dangerous and remote Australian bush. She has said they both were compelled to try to change the world.

From that beginning, they expanded the zoo and branched out into television, film, and books.

But it was television that made them famous. Steve was popular with people of all ages all around the world, telling his fabulous stories as "The Crocodile Hunter" across sixty-four episodes of their same-named series. Among all Discovery Communication networks, their TV show was the second-longest running series.

Many of the episodes also starred Steve's father, Bob, who, along with his wife, had raised his three children at the Beerwah Reptile Park. Bob gave the park to Steve and Terri when they married.

Terri and Steve built on his growing fame and inspirational personality with books and films. The couple created and hosted a children's TV series called *Croc Files* from 1999 to 2001, and then, in 2002, Terri starred with her husband in the movie *The Crocodile Hunter: Collision Course*. The film was based on their television series and was released while the series was still airing. It was also in 2002 that Terri and Steve wrote and published *The Crocodile Hunter: The Incredible Life and Adventures of Steve and Terri Irwin*, a personal recounting of their individual journeys from childhood.

Their worldwide success and fame gave them the ability to advocate for changes in public policy as well as in the hearts and minds of people who previously knew very little about wildlife.

Steve's work with crocodiles first began as an effort to save them after they encroached on the livelihoods and territories of humans. By filming the capture and relocation of crocodiles and other reptiles, he was able to educate people in Australia and around the world. This later involved efforts to conserve the land that the crocodiles lived on. Terri and Steve continued to expand their zoo as another way to protect wildlife, as well as provide a place for research that would help with those efforts.

In 2006, while filming underwater as part of a research expedition, Steve was killed by a stingray barb. Their fourteen years of adventures together ended abruptly, while they were apart.

The media and public response to his sudden death produced countless tributes and outpourings of affection for him and Terri and their two young children. People around the world expressed their shock and grief. Terri has said that this emotional global reaction would have overwhelmed Steve.

She wanted to get a message out to his fans, especially the millions of children who adored him. She told them that everything a hero stands for doesn't end when they die—all that they stood for must continue.

It was a message Terri took to heart.

Since becoming a widow, Terri has continued to live and work in the spotlight while fielding countless questions about her life with Steve. In television interviews she is professional and reserved, even when describing the pain of living without her kindred spirit.

Now, with two grown children—Bindi and Robert—who work alongside her, Terri pushes forward through reality television shows, children's books, and her wildly popular zoo, which she has expanded, and from where she leads her own conservation projects. Having grown up in front of the cameras, Bindi and Robert produce and star in shows about their lives with animals, with each other, and with their famous parents.

Sadly, Terri has become estranged from Steve's father and has said publicly how difficult her grief and those family conflicts have been, and how thankful she is for her foundation of faith.

Terri's books are often quoted, and her thoughts on grief are frequently shared on the internet—as are Bindi's captivating photographs and tweets about her own husband and their daughter, Terri's first granddaughter.

Since Steve's tragic death, living as she does—in the public eye, in the online space, in the multimedia business world, and with wildlife—Terri represents the many young widows who must press on through their grief, keep their complicated lives humming right along, and make it look effortless for their families, friends, and communities around them.

In 2006, she was recognized for "outstanding dedication to wildlife conservation and the tourism industry" and was made an Honorary Member in the General Division of the Order of Australia.

She has been an Australian citizen since 2009, and the family celebrates with all of Australia on Steve Irwin Day, every year on November 15.

In 2013, after six years of leading an environmental campaign against bauxite mining in the ecologically sensitive Steve Irwin Wildlife Reserve, part of her and her husband's legacy of protecting and expanding wild land, Terri was able to stop the eco-damaging mining already underway.

In 2014, a new species of spider was named after her: *Leichhardteus Terriirwinae*.

She received an Honorary Science doctorate from the University of Queensland in 2015, in recognition of her contributions to conservation and environmental management efforts over several decades.

Terri and her family have shared their lives with the public for decades, and are still doing so, including on their zoo website: www.australiazoo.com.au/about-us/the-irwins/.

Throughout her life and her widowhood, Terri has marched on, defending her family, protecting the environment, and speaking out for animals who need a strong voice.

MOOR THOUGHTS ABOUT TERRI IRWIN

Terri Irwin inspires me. I feel a kinship with her, knowing that before her widowhood, she worked alongside her husband in an adventurous, passionate field that brought them joy and excitement both individually and as a loving, caring couple. At home, they created a precious family that gave meaning to the whole of their lives. They worked hard at finding the balance between their professional lives and their family life. My husband and I strived for that same balance.

When I heard the news of Steve's tragic accident in 2006, I immediately thought of how unfair it was. Yes, I knew he'd died doing something he genuinely loved to do, but that didn't change how sad it was, how sudden.

This was the case for my own loss. My husband was young. His accident and death were unexpected. He left behind an adoring wife, very young children, and a bustling business. There was uncertainty about whether the business could continue.

The enormous weight of that kind of intense pain, full-force responsibility, and life shift that Terri was feeling were emotions I was all too familiar with having been in my sixth year of widowhood. Solo parenting as a young businesswoman was a life journey I knew Terri was now about to begin.

Having already faced many important crossroads—deciding on schools for my children, renovating my home after a fire, selling our business and building another interior design firm on my own—I knew the highs and lows that Terri might find herself experiencing. She would learn, as I had learned, that relationships in every area of her life would change and new, unexpected friends would arrive just when she would need them in all areas of her life.

Watching Terri navigate this path with grace and dignity, all while in the public eye, inspired me to keep on keeping on. I knew from watching Terri build her life anew, professionally and personally, that I could—and should—do that too.

I had just finished filming a TLC TV show, *Shalom in the Home*, which led me to being interviewed by Oprah Winfrey on her daytime show. Oprah encouraged me backstage to *do something good with my story*, so with Oprah's words of encouragement and Terri's inspirational light as a guide, I set out to do just that.

Although, I had no idea what that would be.

The show, airing over four years' time, exposed me far and wide, creating excitement, of course, but also an unsettled feeling that I was stuck on Groundhog Day, meaning when people would find me out in the world, they thought my loss had just occurred.

Once, for instance, I was at Ikea in New Jersey and a couple spotted me, walked over, and asked if I was that woman on *Oprah* who had lost her husband on Valentine's Day. I looked up, stunned, and said, "Yes, I am." Then, they asked if they could hug me because their hearts had truly gone out to me when they heard my story. It was a sweet gesture, but also left me wondering how often this sort of thing would happen since I would be unable to control when the show would re-air. This was eight years after my husband died—eight years into my widowhood—and now I could not predict when or who would bring me back to the moment of losing him. I realized that, on some sense of scale, this is the world all widows live in.

"The Oprah Effect," being recognized by strangers for days and weeks, if I'm being honest, caused me to regress. It changed my personality, my willingness to leave the house. When I did go out, I had to brace myself emotionally. It takes courage to step into the big wide world having experienced great loss. It's contraction and expansion occurring at the same time in order to help us grow from our trauma.

I thought of Terri, how hard it must be for someone like her, known and loved worldwide, under that kind of public scrutiny and pressure—in addition to her deep grief and life transitions—to keep marching, head up, smile in place, along that road. Coping with daily struggles. Staying strong and courageous for her children. Knowing that once they're asleep and safe is when the personal demons come out.

She seemed to be an extroverted person like me, so I wondered if she would become more introverted, like I did, to survive the massiveness of the trauma and triggers that are always lurking in the darkness. I wondered if she would struggle with figuring out who she was now without her husband, like I had to. Like Terri, my identity was tied to his, professionally and personally. There was nowhere he was that I was not.

But Terri didn't let the playing out of her widowhood in the public sphere slow her progress, didn't let it stop her march through life. She let her light shine, and her light inspired me to do the same.

I continued to admire her over the years, as she focused on her children first and foremost, paving the way for their legacy to continue and for Steve's to be honored for the positive impact he'd made not just on her life, but also on the lives of his fans worldwide.

She reimagined her life, building on the love and dreams she and Steve had shared and hoped for. She understood that there is a circle of life we're all creating with our choices as we move forward. She knew she was unable to change the past, yet could carry with her what was not lost: the passion, love, and joy she knew with her husband.

Like Terri, I was marching forward through life, creating a legacy for myself in honor of Chad, my late husband, when I made the choice to mentor two widows in my living room and coined our little group as the Modern Widows Club.

The connections we found in Modern Widows Club made sense to us. We had a deep understanding of one another—which was very much how it was with my marriage—so much of what we three widows were feeling didn't need to be said because of our commonalities of meaning and purpose.

Terri's inspirational light helped me understand that the deepest connections remain when a person close to you dies. The body is gone, but the love doesn't die with it. Like Terri, we must decide what to do with the love that remains and in that energy field create something new, a gift for others to receive, a gift for ourselves.

In Terri's life, and my life too, that "creating something new" meant having a mission and purpose that could lead us to change the world in our own way.

When someone visits the Australia Zoo, they can feel the presence of Terri, her late husband, and their children. The same is true when someone is touched by experiencing Modern Widows Club. The collective love we receive is brought forth so others can find comfort, understanding, compassion, and transfigured love. The ripple effect of a million circles.

Both Terri and I have walked the transfiguration pathway to transform outwardly and inwardly into something more beautiful than before, to become elevated and luminous in all we do.

To shine our own lights.

Terri Irwin inspired my heart and mind to live an authentic, luminous life in order to help move humanity forward—and in the process, to move myself and my family forward.

Each of us possesses the power to do this with the gift of our love. I hope you will let Terri's light inspire you to consider finding a way to share all the beautiful love that remains in your life, allowing it to grow and become a force of true good in the world.

QUESTIONS TO CONSIDER

Terri raised her family as a solo parent; it taught her lessons about the circle of life. Do you think about this concept too?

Would you say your widowhood experience is more introverted or extroverted?

Are you changing the world in your own way?

3

BETTY WHITE

The Queen of Improvisation

Actress, comedienne, and America's sweetheart Betty White was an early television pioneer—a fact that is sometimes hard to remember seeing as how she lived much of her long life in the public spotlight. Twice divorced, she was married to her third husband, Allen Ludden, from 1963 until his death in 1981, at age sixty-three. Betty was fifty-nine. She never remarried. When asked why, she said she'd already "had the best." She remained a widow for forty years, until her death on the last day of 2021 at the age of ninety-nine.

White was born in 1922 in Oak Park, Illinois, but her parents moved to Los Angeles, California, when Betty was two. Throughout the 1940s, she performed on various radio shows and, in 1949, began regularly appearing on television, working as a "Girl Friday" on *Hollywood on Television*. She later became host of the show and is considered the first woman to host a talk show.

In 1952, she cofounded Bandy Productions to develop her own projects and from there would go on to break barriers for women in the television industry throughout her lifetime in Hollywood.

She became a frequent guest on television game shows, including *To Tell the Truth*, *What's My Line?*, and *Password*, which was hosted by Allen Ludden, who, of course, became her third husband.

Her breakout role on *The Mary Tyler Moore Show* did not come until she was nearly fifty. During the show's lengthy run in the 1970s, White earned acclaim for her portrayal of Sue Ann Nivens, the sly and flirtatious host of the "Happy Homemaker" show on fictional TV station WJM in Minneapolis, Minnesota. White received three Emmy Award nominations for her work, winning in 1975 and 1976.

White then costarred in the wildly popular television series *The Golden Girls*. Debuting in 1985 (and starring in addition to White, as the innocent and highly optimistic Rose Nylund, Bea Arthur, Rue McClanahan, and Estelle Getty), the series centered on a group of older women, three of whom were widowed and living together in Miami. As Rose, White punctuated heartfelt monologues about her character's belated husband with expert comedic timing.

She earned eight total Emmy nominations and won five awards, including three for either Best Supporting or Best Lead Actress in a Comedy Series, and was inducted into the Television Academy Hall of Fame in 1995.

Her success continued into her eighties and then her nineties, when she joined the cast of *Hot in Cleveland* in 2010. That same year, White also became the oldest host of *Saturday Night Live*—after a Facebook-fueled effort made enough noise to get her on the show.

She hosted and executive produced *Betty White's Off Their Rockers*, which aired from 2012 into 2014. This hidden-camera show featured a mature set of merry pranksters who played jokes on younger generations. White won an Emmy Award nomination for her work on the show in 2012.

She wrote several books during the 1980s and 1990s, including 1987's *Betty White in Person* and 1995's *Here We Go Again: My Life in Television*, which was re-released in 2010. That same year she signed a two-book deal with G.P. Putnam's Sons. White's observations on her life and career, *If You Ask Me (And Of Course You Won't)* was published in the spring of 2011, and her audiobook recording of it won a Grammy Award for best spoken-word album.

In August 2018, PBS aired *Betty White: First Lady of Television*, a retrospective look at her eighty-year career in show business.

But it was never all about show biz for Betty White, who worked with the Los Angeles Zoo and the Morris Animal Foundation for more than four decades. She said she was the luckiest person alive to be able to work in a profession she loved and to work with animals. White was a member of the board of directors of the Greater Los Angeles Zoo Association starting in 1974. Additionally, she served the association as a Zoo Commissioner for eight years. Her book, *My Life at the Zoo: Betty and Her Friends*, was published in 2011.

She shot a video/documentary message to thank fans ahead of what would have been her one hundredth birthday celebration on January 17, 2022. Initially titled, "Betty White: 100 Years Young," it was Betty's thank you to her legion of fans. Sadly, she suffered a stroke on Christmas Day and died on December 31, 2021 at age ninety-nine. The documentary was renamed *Betty White: A Celebration* and was released in theaters in 2022.

White, a groundbreaking television comedienne who showcased her talent across seven decades, helped pave the way for women in comedy with her fearless and unapologetic sense of humor. She defied age stereotypes and, in taking on production responsibilities, shattered gender norms of the day.

In her writings, White shared that she was not afraid of dying, saying that she would improvise when the time came—just as she had so many times in life and work—because some things are better without rehearsal.

MOOR THOUGHTS ABOUT BETTY WHITE

For many, myself included, Betty White was part of our TV life as children and then again as adults. She is proof positive that eighty years in showbiz can have a deep, emotional effect on the national psyche. Many of us, again, me too, were touched by her healing humor. Her exuberance for the joy of life somehow always came through, not only in her dry, candid, and witty comebacks on hit TV shows throughout her career but also in her everyday life.

She was a master at "telling it like it is," no matter how rough-and-tumble it was at that moment, without her audience losing all hope. She made me think a bit broader about big topics that were heavy in emotions, like racism and the unfair treatment of animals, but with a delivery that helped put it into perspective, allowing me to see the issue for myself long after the joke had been delivered. That is empowerment in a nutshell. She was brilliant and talented and empowered me just when I needed empowerment.

I cannot count how many times she has made me light up with laughter watching *The Golden Girls*. It's often said that laughter is the best medicine, and Betty made sure we all had our spoonful of sugar to make it go down so we could all move forward.

Betty was curious and capable, but her courage in the face of resistance is my favorite characteristic of hers. I endeavor to be just like her in this way as well. Through her humor and her life-journey, she gave me an inner confidence to laugh through hard times, to smile at what we cannot control in life and even in death.

Her admiration, friendship, and partnership with her third husband, the great Allen Ludden, imbued her with a high level of love to carry into widowhood and gave her the strength to continue being even more of who she knew herself to be. I try to imagine myself embodying those very same characteristics. She inspires me to do that.

Some of this love became her lifelong commitment to the care of animals. She knew the increased spiritual value of pet therapy long before there were animal rights activists to join that cause. To Betty, it was simply the right thing to believe in, the right way to live your life. I believe she understood animal/human communication better than most. Sort of like she understood how the power of humor and comic relief could help communicate hard topics. She became a light and lively bridge between the world of what people say and how they actually feel. She was brilliant at bringing expression to pain others felt that went unspoken.

I try to emulate Betty in my work and in my life. The example of her courageous widowhood empowers me to share my light and my love, for widows around the world, hearing their voices, understanding their fears, rejoicing in their triumphs, taking on the hard topics with humor to soften the impact.

Like Betty, I strive to stay on course, meeting the hard things head-on with as much wit and grace as possible. What she taught me is that this is often the best way of coping with what we sometimes cannot change, the best way to help heal our spirits and mend our hearts.

Her romantic life with Allen was the envy of many. After his death, she remained a widow for more than forty years, never looking forward with fear, instead carrying their love into her future, grateful for what they'd had, what she would hold on to and never lose. Betty illuminated that love and light in every fiber of her being. She gave us a glimpse of it whenever we saw her on TV.

She lived her life—through three marriages and a long widowhood—as a one-of-a-kind woman with an ever-shining inner light. And so I'm inspired to live my life like that as well. Leading with her picture-perfect smile and her unforgettable sense of humor, Betty White taught me (and many others) about using the power of laughter as a bright healing light for others.

From her I've learned that we can create moments of comic relief if we step out of our own stories and focus our efforts on uplifting others. I think the lesson is to try to shine your inner light like Betty did, that living with laughter just might help you navigate your life-journey over, around, and through the challenges that come your way.

QUESTIONS TO CONSIDER

Betty used laughter to navigate her healing. Have you used laughter to steer yourself through healing?

Can you imagine your own legacy? How do you face your thoughts about your own passing?

Are you able to smile and maintain perspective through hard times?

4

CINDY MCCAIN

A Lifetime Commitment to Service

Confirmed in October, 2021, as the United States representative to the United Nations Agencies for Food and Agriculture, Cindy McCain, widow of presidential candidate and United States Senator John McCain, added diplomat to her inspiring list of lifetime accomplishments, which, in addition to being the powerful wife of a renowned politician, a devoted mother, and a successful businesswoman, includes special needs teacher and humanitarian.

Cindy Hensley was born May 20, 1954, in Phoenix, Arizona, the only child of Marguerite and James Hensley, founder of a beer-distribution company. After obtaining bachelor's and master's degrees in education at the University of Southern California, she began teaching special needs students in Arizona.

In 1979, while on vacation with her parents in Hawaii, she met John McCain. The couple married in 1980 and settled in Arizona in 1981.

When John was elected to the United States House of Representatives in 1982, the couple moved to Washington, D.C. Cindy returned to Arizona in 1984 after a series of miscarriages and because she felt like an outsider in the United States capital city, where John's ex-wife was popular among Washingtonians. Back in her home state, Cindy gave birth to the couple's daughter, Meghan, that same year. The McCains later had two sons and adopted a second daughter from Bangladesh.

In 1988, Cindy founded the American Voluntary Medical Team (AVMT), a nonprofit that provided medical care throughout the world. She personally led more than fifty excursions to deliver aid and supplies.

Her life journey has not always been easy. Indeed, her strength was greatly tested in the late 1980s when she became addicted to prescription painkillers (to alleviate pain after two spinal surgeries for ruptured discs) and eventually admitted to stealing medication from the AVMT. With the help of her family, McCain battled and beat her addiction, took full responsibility for her mistake, and eventually became comfortable telling the story of her addiction and recovery.

In the 1990s and 2000s, she worked with numerous humanitarian groups, including Operation Smile, CARE, and the HALO Trust, an organization dedicated to removing landmines. She publicly supported same-sex marriage when it was a challenging decision for her to do so and was deeply involved in efforts to end human trafficking.

When her father died in 2000, she became chairman of Hensley & Co. That same year, she campaigned for her husband John's Republican presidential bid, where he was defeated by George W. Bush in the Republican primary. In 2004, she suffered a stroke and recovered in Coronado, California. Then, she supported John's memorable second presidential bid in 2007, where he was defeated by Barack Obama in the United States general election.

In 2017, Senator McCain was diagnosed with glioblastoma, a malignant brain tumor. The severity of the illness led to the possibility that John would not be able to finish his term in office and that the Governor of Arizona would have to appoint a successor until a special election could be held. There is a political practice known as "Widow's Succession" in which a spouse may be named as her husband's interim replacement. However, Cindy indicated she was not interested in public office, and after John's death on August 18, 2018, their friend, former Arizona Senator Jon Kyl, was appointed to complete her husband's term.

In 2019, showing the independence and courage of her husband, Cindy stated that the Republican party was no longer the party that she and John had known and worked tirelessly for, and on September 22, 2020, she endorsed Joe Biden's bid for the presidency. Subsequently, she became a member of the advisory board of the Biden-Harris Transition Team, providing advice on women's and children's issues.

Cindy published a memoir of her life with John in April 2021 entitled *Stronger: Courage, Hope, and Humor in My Life with John McCain*. She refers to her thirty-eight-year marriage as an adventure. When the book was released, she said, "Because of what I learned from him about honor and courage, I know how to use my voice to stand up for what I believe is best for me, my family, and America. Writing *Stronger* at this time was important to me, and I'm excited to share the full story of our life together."

After just six months on the job as United States ambassador to the United Nations Agencies for Food and Agriculture, Russia invaded Ukraine. In a May 2022 interview with Politico, McCain spoke about the world food crisis resulting from the Russian invasion. In addition to working with other countries and the United Nations to stop food blockades, address grain shortages, and restart farming in Ukraine, there was another aspect to McCain's role as ambassador: keeping the American public informed about what was actually going on, and why it was important to help address food insecurity.

In 2020, Cindy McCain became a grandmother for the third

time when daughter Meghan gave birth to Liberty Sage, Cindy's first granddaughter.

From Arizona rodeo queen, to wife of a politician, to widow, to humanitarian, to ambassador, to proud and loving mother and grandmother, Cindy McCain has truly let her light burn bright throughout her marriage, her widowhood, and her inspiring life journey.

MOOR THOUGHTS ABOUT CINDY MCCAIN

For me, Cindy McCain's life story is remarkable not simply because of her impressive achievements, which are extraordinary indeed, but because her journey, putting aside her public renown, is so emotionally relatable to many modern widows, myself included.

Businesswoman, wife, mother (both biological and by adoption), grandmother, widow, diplomat, First Lady of Arizona, humanitarian, and ambassador for the United States. These are Cindy's life-resume entries. Lofty as they are, within them I recognize the emotional challenges she faced navigating the ever-changing landscape between private and public life—a journey she gracefully negotiates to this day. But her most relevant and most inspirational quality, I think, is her *resilience* through those many seasons of life.

A resilience, a light, she found through the power of love.

Cindy found both love and a home when she met John. She then stood strong by her man in life, through two presidential campaigns, and in death. We've all seen Cindy in the news and know the story of her marriage to John, but until I traveled to Arizona myself, I didn't know the true power of her journey.

In 2022, I began researching this strong woman and brave widow who has risen above the mindless chatter to focus her efforts on making the world a better place in geographically less fortunate areas of the world. I discovered that her ability to step into a troubling situation, internalize its complex and dynamic inner workings, and offer smart and heartfelt solutions was a result of her having lived a life fully focused on compassion. Caring deeply for others' well-being, putting their needs before hers, is what gives her the strength of purpose to carry on, to be resilient when all feels lost.

It is a life philosophy I have chosen to emulate. Like Cindy, I care about women's and children's issues worldwide—widows and fatherless children specifically. Cindy began as a special needs educator, understanding that the crucial first years of a child's life set a lifelong trajectory of either security and love or, sadly, the absence of those qualities. As an only child with parents who were "all in," raising their daughter in a stable home overflowing with love, I imagine Cindy understood that she had enough love in her heart to support others in need of emotional support.

Cindy's sense of compassion, the urgency in her heart to help others as quickly as possible, is supported by research that shows early childhood care is critical, especially within the first seven years of a child's life. I know this to be true firsthand.

Like many modern widows, I felt the heavy responsibility of sudden solo parenting, since both of my daughters were under the age of four when their father died in a hit-and-run car accident. Losing my husband and best friend was my primary loss. Losing my parenting partner was my difficult secondary loss. I experienced the devastating impacts of survivor's guilt, PTSD, grief, depression, loneliness and anxiety, all while caring for small children whose needs were in my hands. Their security and need for my love required that I, a widow, a mother in crisis, find support specific to my needs.

Unfortunately, I didn't receive all the help I needed. It simply wasn't available or was too hard to find. That's why, today, I'm so passionate about creating a new generation of widow mentors, leaders, and advocates to champion widows' causes. We are doing better, so that's very good news, but there's still so much more work to do in improving how women are supported during their widowhood.

Inspirational role models such as Cindy, who use resilience powered by love, helped me understand the immediacy demanded when love and light are needed.

Cindy has always known that early intervention mattered. It's evident in her involvement in founding the American Voluntary Medical Team, a nonprofit that provided medical care throughout the world and led more than fifty excursions to deliver aid and supplies. Families in need have kids in need.

Cindy's book *Stronger: Courage, Hope, and Humor in My Life with John McCain* is a beautiful love story full of the stuff legends and legacies are made of: strength, courage, hope, and humor.

Like Cindy, I believe living one's best life—your life, my life, the lives of all women, widows, and children—is worth honoring, worth fighting for with love and strength. Like Cindy, I believe that family, honor, love, and legacy are values worth shining your light on. As a modern widow, you too can honor your life and the lives of your children—the life you're living now—beyond the sudden loss or illness or incapacity of your beloved, beyond your inability to change what is, what can't be changed. Because what has *not* changed is the love that is eternal and ever-present. Love that empowered Cindy to be resilient, to move forward and find purpose by reaching back to others with courage and, yes, love. My husband is with me still, every step of the way. I feel certain that John is with Cindy.

Someday when I meet Cindy, I hope she will know how inspired I have been by her courage to reinvent herself decade after decade, to use the power of love to be resilient through the hills and valleys of life as she blazes new trails for herself and those around her. I look forward to hearing her speak about how she continues to define her journey as what I call: "A woman of fulfilled marriage, a widow, promise made, promise kept, promise honored."

Curiously, our daughters share the same name, though with different spellings: Meghan (McCain) and Meagan (Moor). It's a name with Greek origins meaning *pearl* or *great* or *mighty*. I find it interesting that a pearl is made inside a mollusk shell only when an irritant enters. In order for the oyster to create the pearl —as a way of protecting itself—it covers the foreign substance with nacre (mother of pearl), eventually turning the irritant into a thing of love and beauty, a pearl.

QUESTIONS TO CONSIDER

Cindy uses her voice to stand up for what she believes in. What have you found in widowhood that you want to use your voice for?

Do you feel stronger in some ways now that you know the experience of widowhood?

How has family played a role in your building a new life for yourself?

5

KATHARINE MEYER GRAHAM

Publishing Empire Pioneer

Katharine Meyer was born June 16, 1917, into wealth and privilege. She was the daughter, the fourth of five children, of Eugene Meyer, a second-generation Jewish American (who became a successful businessman in California, on Wall Street in New York City, and in Washington, D.C.) and a nominally Lutheran mother, Agnes, who Katharine described as having no mothering instincts. Indeed, Katharine and her siblings were reared by the nannies, nurses, and teachers who lived with them—and shielded them from anti-Semitism. Later, looking back on her incredible journey, Katharine reflected on the role that chance and luck played in her life.

Katharine didn't know to describe her upbringing as isolated. She and one sister grew up separate from their older siblings, and to Katharine that was simply normal. She was sent to school whether healthy or ill and, growing up in her father's large house staffed by cooks, housekeepers, and others, learned precious little about self-sufficiency. Looking back later, as an adult with her own four children, she realized that her untreated lingering childhood cough had likely been tuberculosis.

Katharine's mother, Agnes, was a great beauty, a bohemian intellectual who entertained often, at both the family's seven-hundred-acre Upstate New York property and at their Washington D.C. mansion, where she hosted the politicians, artists, and business leaders of her time. She had a brilliant mind and became a writer in an era when women were expected to become homemakers, with professional exceptions for teachers and nurses. She hadn't been born into wealth and also hadn't earned it, as her husband, Eugene, had. Yet despite a suspicious streak that presented as selfish, Agnes took full advantage of Eugene's money and provided tennis, music, and riding lessons for herself and her children.

Katharine was awed by and terrified of her mother, too scared to disobey her. With such strong modeling, "suspicious and selfish" became part of Katharine's makeup too. As an adult, she regretted having those traits and said that she overcame those tendencies when she married Phil Graham, who was exceedingly generous.

While Katharine was still in high school, her father anonymously purchased *The Washington Post* at a bankruptcy auction. In a town with five newspapers, the *Post* was number five. With declining circulation and a bottom line in the red, the *Post* took all of Eugene's attention just two weeks after he'd retired from Wall Street. Though Katharine was not close to him when she was a child, he somehow conveyed his belief in her, encouraging her as she attended Vassar, and later the University of Chicago.

While at college, Katharine had almost no knowledge of how to live in the world, even to the point of not realizing that she needed to find a way to have her clothes laundered. Her clean clothes had always materialized, in the same way that dresses suddenly appeared after her mother had done the shopping for her. Fortunately, her college friends were a diverse group who helped her then and, for many of them, for the rest of her life.

This "group atmosphere" became a college way of life that appealed to Katharine. A way of life she would create again years later in Washington, D.C.

Her father Eugene was well-connected in both business and government circles, having managed the United States Federal Reserve as an appointee of President Herbert Hoover, and Katharine rode his considerable coattails, working at small newspapers in New York and California until following her father to the *Post* in Washington, D.C.

In 1939, the United States capital was populated with young idealistic law graduates who were remaking the city with their hope and enthusiasm for President Franklin D. Roosevelt and his New Deal programs.

With small government salaries and big dreams, Katharine and her friends shared expenses, all of them living the group-atmosphere life she'd enjoyed in college. She's described these days as a time, like the John F. Kennedy years later, when youth could accomplish a lot, with ideas percolating and being listened to by those in authority.

Katharine and her friends' idea of fun was to debate policy and argue with each other frequently at the big house that was the scene of countless late-night discussions of their days as law clerks, government workers, and, in Katharine's case, a newspaper writer. As the daughter of the publisher, she kept a low profile, writing mainly feature-style editorials, not making waves, doing her job and doing it well.

She met Phil Graham at one of these rowdy intellectual salons. He was engaged to a law student and was a clerk for Felix Frankfurter, a United States Supreme Court Justice. Their work and social lives spilled over into each other, overlapping through journalism, law, and government.

She and Phil happened to be the only two of their group without dates on New Year's Eve, 1939, and spent the evening exchanging stories. A few weeks later, they were again the only two in their crowd without dinner plans. Their relationship leaped forward.

At age twenty-five, Phil was intelligent, charming, affable, and funny, Katharine later shared.

He was not eager to meet her wealthy parents after a courtship of only a few months. Phil's father had sacrificed to send him to law school and expected him to return to the family dairy farm in the agricultural land west of Miami, Florida. Formerly swampland, the area had been home to his small family since 1921.

Phil's parents had worked hard and argued constantly. His mother, a teacher, had died of cancer when he was nineteen and away in college. Deeply affected by grief—and by the years of their loud conflicts—Phil had a no-argument rule in the home, which prevented many normal discussions and joint decisions. He'd changed schools often as the family moved and was usually the wittiest one in class, according to classmates. He was also a hard-drinking country boy who helped his father in unsuccessful political campaigns.

Justice Frankfurter was a longtime friend of the Meyer family and gave his formal approval of their marriage in an era when law clerks were expected to remain single so that they could also serve as drivers and work regular late-night schedules.

Though she didn't know how to cook eggs or do laundry yet, Katharine had learned enough to design her wedding gown, made-to-order at Bergdorf Goodman in New York. Another longtime family friend, the photographer Edward Steichen, brought his camera to the small ceremony.

Phil insisted that they live as their contemporaries lived, on their own small salaries, but Katharine stocked her closet and bought furnishings while still supported by her parents.

She began noticing his drinking problem during these early years. She suffered a miscarriage and had a child who died immediately after he was born. They watched as Europe began to become inflamed by war, and Phil joined the Army. With the privilege of her upbringing, she was able to follow him to his training sites in South Dakota and elsewhere. She moved to small towns that suddenly became cities with the influx of trainees. This was when Katharine learned about dealing with all kinds of people, something Phil had learned in rural Florida at a much younger age.

He worked behind the scenes in the government war effort. She kept his long letters from his duty assignments overseas, treasuring his descriptions of his love for her and his plans for their life together. She described their early years together as a happy time and wrote that she grew up considerably as he led her down paths different from those of her parents. He countered her resistance to new ideas with laughter, gaiety, and originality. He also invested time with her parents and became close to them, overcoming his initial apprehensions about their wealth and tendency to control their children.

Her father soon began to recruit Phil to work at the *Post*. Though it was a time when fathers were expected to pass their businesses to their sons, Eugene turned to his son-in-law after his own son showed no interest in the paper. It didn't occur to any of them to consider Katharine, even though she had worked in the newspaper industry for years by then, as had her mother.

Phil took over as publisher after only five months at *The Washington Post*. At the age of thirty, he replaced his father-in-law as the head of a small paper struggling with circulation and finances.

During the next twenty years, Phil's perpetually sunny persona turned manic. He returned to alcoholism and was eventually diagnosed with a bipolar disorder, during a time when electric shock therapy was the typical treatment. He began a long-term affair, left Katharine and their adult children, and forced friends and family to take sides in a battle for the paper.

He refused medical treatment and suffered for years before taking his own life at their home. Katharine would never forget the sound of the gunshot and its aftermath.

Her battles moved to the newsroom as she fought off hostile offers to purchase *The Washington Post*. Finding comfort and challenge at work, she dove in deeper. Having always been among the rich and powerful, she worked hard to remain neutral in the editorial processes of her publications—at least until Richard Nixon's presidency, when the *Post* broke the news about the Watergate break-in and then famously followed the story to its conclusion.

Her years of leadership at *The Washington Post* are well-documented. She was strong in the face of fierce resistance, brave when the times required great courage, steady when the political winds were howling.

What is often forgotten in Katharine's incredible story is that she weathered these storms as a widow.

She had spent years eavesdropping in her father's drawing room as he debated with leaders in business and government. She was soon watching and learning from her own home in Washington, on the sidelines and the tarmacs during war, moving closer and closer to the front row of history until she became an important part of it.

While letting her brilliant light shine as a widow, Katharine Meyer Graham changed American history through her support of her investigative journalists during the *Post's* persistent Watergate reporting.

MOOR THOUGHTS ABOUT KATHARINE MEYER GRAHAM

For me and for many other women, Katharine's life story has all the elements of a great movie: a courageous heroine battling shifting social tides, economic change, family addiction, troubled marriage, lost pregnancies, shifting political winds, and widowhood while figuring out and then refiguring out who she was and what she had to do to survive the chaos around her. She believed in luck but learned happenstance could only take her so far and discovered that hard work would be the key to her survival.

Given the luck of her birthright, her privileged yet isolated childhood, her confusion navigating the wider world when she left home to gain an education, the challenges of her marriage, and her whirlwind, ultimately historic newspaper career, the fact that she understood hard work was her way forward and then acted on that fact to forge her path is what makes her an inspiration for me as a working woman and widow.

One aspect of Katharine's life journey I admire is that she could have waltzed through life, dancing on her father's coattails, but chose another, more challenging road to travel. She may not have known how to do her own laundry or cook a meal for herself—she'd lived with doting maids and cooks her entire life to that point in time—but she knew she wanted to learn, knew she wanted to be an independent woman, and so made the decision to work hard and stay strong until she could do those things, find herself, and thrive on her own terms.

How she traveled that road is inspirational for me as a working woman and modern widow. Katharine grew up having many of the practical parts of life already attended to, so she had more time to focus on the people around her, to develop her emotional intelligence and build a kind of inner strength that allowed her to read between the lines of words and behavior. This inner strength, this light, fostered within her a desire to grow and succeed in spite of the fact that growing and succeeding wasn't required of her, to use her light to help those around her succeed and grow. I strive to live like that, to work hard and focus on the people around me, helping them grow and succeed as a way of helping myself.

By the time she stepped into her role at *The Washington Post*, I feel she'd reached the tipping point of believing she had nothing left to lose. Certainly, it had to have been an overwhelming moment for her, yet it seems she felt prepared—intuitively—for the challenges ahead. She followed her inner light during those first dark days and nights. Memories guided her. She found her footing and came into her own in front of the world as the publisher and leader of a powerful newspaper.

It's a survival lesson worth learning—that using the inspirational moments from your past can help guide you through your present and lead you to your future. It's a lesson I took to heart as I moved forward in my widowhood, creating the Modern Widows Club, and earning what I like to call my PhD in Uncommon Knowledge.

By her example, Katharine teaches us something more. That, yes, work can bring solace to grief, acting as a distraction that provides purpose. Like Katharine, I often ask myself where I should invest my time—both actual and emotional—to receive the best possible post-loss return on my investment. Katharine intuitively knew that this important, reflective process was critical to surviving her widowhood. The same has been true for me and would be true, I now know firsthand, for many other widows.

Ultimately, to survive my widowhood, I made the choice to put my interior design career on hold for a year and a half in order to stabilize home life for my two young daughters—and for myself, if truth be told—as best I could.

No one knows what the right next choice is when their life unexpectedly implodes. That widowhood is hard is the only thing we know for sure. For me, in the beginning, grieving and loving my children in between paying the bills was just about all I could manage. Grieving is exhausting.

And then I found meaningful work to do. Interior design kept calling, and after eighteen months, I went back to work. It was difficult at first. The brain fog of widowhood made it hard to remember the million details of design. And, of course, I missed working with my husband as much as I missed him at home.

But knowing that Katharine had experienced this same sense of loss and had overcome it with strength of purpose and a focus on helping those around her helped me move forward through my challenges. I very much believe this happens for almost all widows. Strength of purpose and focus on helping others. A lesson not to be forgotten.

Katharine became a light in her industry. Many found the truth in her articles and were inspired as she summoned the strength and stepped up to be the boldest of publishers during a national crisis. Again, Katharine is a bright example of how a modern widow can find her way to make a positive impact in her world by shining her inner light so that others may find their way safely home.

Clearly, as a modern widow and working mother, I'm inspired by Katharine's life story. Her hardship was surprising given her upper-class beginnings, but it was that hardship—

including and perhaps especially the challenges of her widowhood—that forced her to find her inner strength, by working hard and focusing on those around her. Like Katharine, I work hard at helping others through the Modern Widows Club. I feel sure this is a way forward for many modern widows.

QUESTIONS TO CONSIDER

Katharine felt isolation in her life and distance from others. How do you manage those feelings in widowhood?

There are many changes that occur when becoming a new widow. Are there areas that were completely foreign to you, and yet you found a way through them?

Influencers and mentors are important in this new life stage. Have you had any special motivators or inspirational people in your experience that you could thank for making a big impact on your life?

CORETTA SCOTT KING

Activism Rooted in Nonviolence

In 1927, Coretta Scott was born the middle child of an Alabama farm family living in a two-room house. When she was old enough to attend school, her day began with caring for the animals and tending the vegetable garden before going to class. She learned early in her life about racism when a white man set fire to the sawmill her father had recently purchased. The ugly event filled Coretta with rage, but her mother, Bernice, taught her children to rise above violent incidents.

She had much to rise above. Indeed, Coretta's life was filled with racial inequities. Though white children rode a bus, Coretta, her sister, and her brother walked three miles to their overcrowded, understaffed, racially separated school. Required to buy their own textbooks, many Black children were unable to continue their attendance. But Coretta worked after school and weekends, took her studies seriously, and graduated at the top of her class. Her reward was a ten-mile commute to high school.

Walking was no longer an option. So she and her sister moved in with a Black family—paying room and board—in order to live closer to the school.

Upon graduation, she joined her sister at Antioch College in Ohio, and quickly realized that her rural Alabama schooling had not prepared her for the rigors of higher education. She also noticed that not all of her classmates had the same passion about equal education and other racial issues. Her fight expanded to include these as well.

She became active in the National Association for the Advancement of Colored People (NAACP) while still in college, remained a serious student, focused on a career in music, and graduated in 1951.

Through a mutual friend, she met Martin Luther King, Jr., a Baptist minister studying for a PhD in theology and philosophy, and the young couple forged an immediate connection.

"You have everything I have ever wanted in a wife," King told her on their first date in 1952.

Coretta was moved by King's strong sense of right and wrong, by his unshakeable moral foundation. His nonviolent philosophy and approach to the problems they encountered followed the same principles that her parents had taught her back in Alabama. The couple married in 1953, and Coretta set aside her plans for a singing career and focused on motherhood, creating a home, and building a life with Reverend King.

King became the minister at Dexter Avenue Baptist Church in Montgomery, Alabama, and he and Coretta had the first of their four children. It was then that history arrived at their doorstep.

Rosa Parks, the Montgomery bus boycott, and increasing strife in the community soon resulted in a bomb being thrown onto the Kings' front porch. No one was injured. And no one flinched.

As the years passed, Coretta used her singing talents to raise money for the civil rights movement. She hosted Freedom Concerts for the Southern Christian Leadership Conference and gained her own reputation in the civil rights arena, attending the Women's Strike for Peace in Geneva, Switzerland, in 1962.

In her book *My Life with Martin Luther King, Jr.* she describes these early years. And, of course, King's story has also been told by biographers, filmmakers, reporters, and through his powerful speeches.

Protesting Jim Crow laws and the war in Vietnam, King expanded his message and frequently tackled the underlying reasons for poverty.

He also foretold his own death, telling Coretta that he didn't expect to live a long life, urging her to be prepared to continue on, to continue the march after he was gone.

After his tragic assassination on April 4, 1968, Coretta recalled asking herself what is was that she was supposed to do now that Martin was gone. Her answer was: *More!*

The nation watched as the young widow with four small children held up a community in mourning while also facing down those who were not sympathetic to the Kings' cause. Many people responded with violence, and reactions of more violence, when King was assassinated. Rioting took place in more than 125 cities, resulting in more than forty deaths. King had persisted in spreading his message of nonviolence through peaceful marches despite his opponents' bombings and attacks on Sunday School children.

In April 1968, she delivered a speech in Memphis prior to the march he'd promised to lead, challenging King's mourners to… "see that his spirit never dies," also saying, "How many men must die before we can really have a free and true and peaceful society?"

Her question reverberates even today.

That same week, Coretta was on the cover of *Life* magazine, where she was described as a grieving widow, veiled and beautiful.

Three weeks later, she gave a moving speech in New York's Central Park, saying, "I come to you in my grief only because you keep alive the work and dreams for which my husband gave his life."

Her words moved millions.

Coretta continued to lead the fight for equality under the law, picking up where King left off, not looking to his past accomplishments but making his vision her own, adding her powerful light to the movement. In Atlanta, the establishment of The King Center, for instance, was an immediate result of her indefatigable spirit, of her unshakeable resolve to help shape the future.

To this day, the King Center houses more than one million documents and provides programs to train and aid people striving for nonviolent social change around the world. Exhibits, conferences, and workshops carry forward King's message of freedom, justice, and peace.

Coretta also worked for years to help create a federal holiday to honor her husband. Though established into law in 1984, some states chose (and still choose) to honor others on Martin Luther King, Jr. Day, including Confederate General Robert E. Lee.

Which meant her work was not done. Coretta continued answering the call for justice by creating coalitions and meeting with people in Europe, Africa, Asia, and Latin America as well as throughout the United States.

She was honored by the Academy of Achievement in 1997, sharing with those gathered that when she and Martin got married, she married not only the man she loved, but the cause as well. Without this kind of commitment, she could not have continued after Martin's death.

For more than forty years, Coretta steadfastly delivered the message of nonviolence, and expanded it to include urgent encouragement to women.

Only six years after her husband's violent death, the family's matriarch, her mother-in-law, Mrs. Martin Luther King, Sr., was assassinated at Ebenezer Baptist Church in Atlanta. Grieving the death of Alberta King, her mother-in-law, Coretta and her children again had to rise above the violence, as her own mother had taught her. To that end she said, "Women, if the soul of the nation is to be saved, I believe that you must become its soul."

She later became a supporter of gay rights, sometimes called "the new civil rights." Though there is little evidence of her husband's feelings about this or women's rights, Coretta let her light shine bright and said, "...I appeal to everyone who believes in Martin Luther King, Jr.'s dream to make room at the table of brotherhood and sisterhood for lesbian and gay people."

This love for all humanity continues to be evidenced in Occupy Wall Street, the Black Lives Matter movement, and in anti-war protests, even without the name of either King in the news accounts. Their four children continue the work at the King Center and sometimes disagree with their parents' stands and with each other's.

Perhaps that is the brightest result of Coretta's fearless light. That disagreement does not necessitate violence. That peace and love build the bridge to equality and justice.

MOOR THOUGHTS ABOUT CORETTA SCOTT KING

Like Coretta, I am a middle child. I have felt this connection with her for a long time. Like me, I feel sure she knew what it meant to be at the center of a family balancing act. But unlike me, a Caucasian girl growing up in Arkansas, looking from the outside in at the segregated and racist environment so prevalent in the South and beyond, Coretta was forced to live that confusing and concerning reality firsthand, all day, every day.

Coretta and her husband shared a purpose: to raise up a movement. To that end, they empowered each other every step of the way. I had this experience with my late husband as well, although our purpose was less noble and without the risk of real danger: to succeed in the business of architecture and interior design. But at least on some level, our purposes were parallel. Coretta and her husband helped people build better lives, and my husband and I helped people build better homes to live those lives within.

It's not the same thing, of course. But it's a connection with her I hold on to.

In my teen years, I learned about Coretta and Dr. Martin Luther King, Jr. in my history classes. Then I looked around and saw how white my own world really was: at school, church, and within my circles of friends.

Around this time, my parents began to talk to us about racial differences and injustices. My father hired a Black auto mechanic who was also a pastor. We were invited to attend their African American church, an experience that to this day is one of the best memories of my childhood.

The families in this church worshiped with joy and love, singing in the aisles, opening their hearts to everyone who walked through the church doors. Faith was the air they breathed. I experienced a new world, and it lit a spark inside of me.

Although Coretta was not in that particular church at that moment in time, looking back now, I realize her legacy was in every smiling face that welcomed me. I was humbled by this level of unconditional acceptance and favor by people society insisted were different from me.

But I wasn't different. And they weren't different. We were all the same in the eyes of God. This, I learned later, was Coretta's message that fueled her purpose.

When I learned more about Coretta and Dr. Martin Luther King, Jr.'s mission, there was something about her that struck me as phenomenal: her willingness to be the face of resistance, to be a cultural disruptor in support of others being treated unfairly. She was an inspirational warrior for justice and decency.

I like to think we would have been on the same side of history if our timing had been aligned. I like to believe I would have walked alongside her, helping her illuminate the need to treat all people as beautiful—no matter the color of their skin. I like to imagine we would have been fast friends in the name of nonviolence, love, and inner light.

In widowhood especially, I took her message and let it empower *my* purpose. I let her inspire me to be strong when I'm frustrated and disheartened by what I see happening with widows around the world: unnoticed and unaddressed child-bride marriages; unprotected fatherless daughters filling the wellspring of the human trafficking industry; forced cultural widow-cleansing rituals; widow disinheritance; widows called witches and neglected in places of worship, governments and society.

I've been told that my anger toward these and other injustices is not lady-like. That I should sit down and calm down. But I won't do either, partly because Coretta didn't when she—and her husband—were told the same.

I let Coretta's light shine in me, speaking up against the odds, determined to continue on my path of purpose.

I relate to her sadness of loss, her rough road of widowhood. Yet every morning, when the sun came up, Coretta recommitted to the mission she shared with her husband. She knew who she was and what she was capable of. She knew pain and could not stand by to see it being inflicted so unfairly. I share this sentiment with her, as many widows no doubt do. Deep pain can reshape you as a peacemaker—if you let your inner light shine.

Coretta did just that, which is why her mission expanded to the LGBTQ community and to women's rights. Her ability to expand her loving nature in the face of hate is the epitome of fearlessness. I try hard to embody this spirit when faced with setbacks and disappointments. Coretta's courage, her light, is still an inspiration for me.

Coretta lived by values we rarely see shining so brightly in today's world. I try hard to live her values, lighting a path so others can rekindle their light, to help them bear the unbearable and in so doing become transcendent, more beautiful than before.

I make every effort to live like I share Coretta's spirit and courage, like a woman who can hold the soul of a nation, like a woman who believes in prevailing grace in action, like a woman —a widow—who wants to forge a world where all can find freedom and experience peace, justice, and opportunity.

I do this for widows when I advocate and will continue to do so for the rest of my life, bringing Coretta with me to help me forge peace, never being silenced about the dire lives of so many widows, understanding and sharing their grief experiences, their phenomenal propensity for hope, growth, and empowerment.

Change comes when we are courageous enough to give our whole self to the betterment of others, repairing the world, in my case shouting out the voiceless cries of the widowed women who must be heard, knowing that being a bridge builder is the lightmaker's way forward.

Lightmakers know the feeling of being in the dark night of the soul. Pain teaches lessons like nothing else can. Coretta became a light in the darkness, bringing necessary change to other souls seeking peace and light and love and acceptance. I honor her path and allow myself to be inspired by it. It has helped me heal in the deepest of ways. I wholeheartedly recommend you consider the same.

QUESTIONS TO CONSIDER

Coretta felt that she was called to "see his spirit never dies". Is there a way you are ensuring your loved one's spirit never dies?

Has your pain taught you life lessons you plan to share with others?

Have you experienced inequities as a widow that you hope to advocate for changing?

7

GRAÇA MACHEL

Global Leadership for Peace and Human Rights

Graça Simbine was born on October 17, 1945, only seventeen days after the death of her father. She was the youngest of six children who grew up in rural Incadine, Mozambique (which was then Portuguese East Africa). She is best known today as Graça Machel because of her marriage to Nelson Mandela. But long before she met the former president of South Africa, she was a leader in her neighboring home country of Mozambique. A freedom fighter, highly regarded educator, philanthropist, and national leader, Graça is destined to take her place in history as a tireless worker for justice, education, and social equality.

When young Graça earned a scholarship to attend high school in the Mozambique capital city of Maputo, she was the only Black African in a class of forty whites. In an interview later in life, she recalled wondering why she felt like a stranger in her own country—they were the foreigners, not her—and recognizing that something wasn't right.

She excelled at the local Methodist mission schools and then the University of Lisbon, Portugal, on a mission scholarship. She studied German at the university, and began to work toward independence for her nation. Outspoken against the Portuguese colonial government, Graça led the call for change and freedom from Mozambique's colonial rulers.

In 1973, she joined the Mozambique Liberation Front (FRELIMO) and focused on teaching, first in FRELIMO-held areas in the province of Cabo Delgado and thereafter at the FRELIMO School in Tanzania. She also worked with women and children's groups, beginning a lifetime of advocacy. She became Deputy Director of the FRELIMO Secondary School in Bagamoyo, Tanzania, in 1974.

Mozambique's independence from Portugal was achieved in June 1975. Graça was appointed Mozambican Minister of Education and Culture, a post she held until 1989. During this time, the percentage of children who attended primary and secondary schools more than doubled for boys and nearly doubled for girls.

Her first husband was Samora Machel, the first president of Mozambique; they had two children during their eleven-year marriage. In 1986, she was widowed for the first time when Samora died in a plane crash under unknown circumstances during a period of political turmoil. Pictures of the funeral show her bowing over her husband's casket, stricken with grief. She dressed in black for five years.

In 1991, prompted by her twelve-year-old son, she restarted her public career. As the young, glamorous, tragic First Lady of Mozambique, she was often compared to Jackie Kennedy, the former First Lady of the United States.

Once a freedom fighter and now a young widow, she turned her energies to improving the lives of women and children in Mozambique. She worked to relocate displaced orphans and empower women in her capacity as Chairman of National Organization of Children of Mozambique.

Her work in Mozambique led to service as President of

UNESCO's National Commission in Mozambique. She was one of the delegates of the UNICEF Conference in 1988 and was also on the steering committee of the World Conference on Education for All in 1990.

In addition to her native Shangaan language (Xitsonga), Graça also spoke Spanish, French, Italian, Portuguese, and English, making her imminently qualified and comfortable at international forums that included presidents and royalty. Her ready smile and self-effacing humor were frequently remarked upon.

Her lifelong passion for youth education continued, taking her into service as an expert on children's issues for the United Nations. Graça continued her dedication to the issue of child marriage through the organization Girls Not Brides: The Global Partnership to End Child Marriage, an international, nongovernmental organization to end child marriage around the world. As an international champion for children, she authored the book *The Impact of War on Children*.

Through this work, she met Nelson Rolihlahla Mandela, the South African anti-apartheid revolutionary and political leader. He served as the first president of independent South Africa from 1994 to 1999. Ideologically an African nationalist and socialist, he had led the African National Congress party from 1991 to 1997.

Their first meeting, after Mandela's release from prison in 1990, was at a very low point in his life. Graça has said they were both very lonely and in need of someone to talk to, someone who could understand. In private, Mandela was broken. His wife, Winnie, refusing him any marital relationship, had humiliated him in public during their celebrity divorce.

He was South Africa's first Black head of state and the first Black national elected in a fully representative democratic election. His government focused on dismantling the legacy of apartheid by tackling institutionalized racism and fostering racial reconciliation.

When they married in 1998, Graça was fifty-two, his third wife. South Africans were well-acquainted with his ex-wife Winnie Mandela. His first marriage ended, he has said, when he'd had to choose between the commitments a marriage demands and his activism. South Africans were protective of their beloved icon, whose everyday conversations were quoted and published.

Graça later said their maturity made some things easier. While Mandela wooed her, she remained in the background, allowing South Africans to fall in love with her too.

Mandela once said Graça made him "bloom like a flower." Despite her reluctance to marry him at first, they became inseparable after their small private wedding on his eightieth birthday.

Her marriage to Mandela makes her the only woman in modern history to have served as first lady of two countries: Mozambique and South Africa.

She was widowed for the second time when Mandela died in 2013 at age ninety-five. Graça recalled that, "When he left he said, 'I leave you in peace, and I want you to live in peace.' On the day of his passing, I was not able to think, I was numb. Looking back, I imagine him tall and proud, walking, and all of them rising to welcome him."

In her second widowhood, she continues to fight for human rights through universities and international organizations. She received a United Nations award and has been made an honorary Dame Commander of the Order of the British Empire. From 1999 to 2019, she served as Chancellor of the University of Cape Town, South Africa's legislative capital.

She is a founding member of The Elders, an independent group of former global leaders formed in 2007 by Nelson Mandela to work together for peace and human rights. She also held the position of President of the School for Oriental and African Studies (SOAS) at the University of London and is Chancellor of the African Leadership University in Kigali, Rwanda.

In 2006, she was conferred an honorary doctorate of Humane

Letters by the University of Massachusetts, among many other awards such as InterAction's humanitarian award in 1997; World's Children's Prize along with Mandela in 2005; and a major award from CARE.

In 2010, she founded the Graça Machel Trust to help promote and strengthen women's leadership and children's rights, furthering her dream of a free African nation where every citizen has opportunities.

As recently as July 2022, her work with the trust took her to the world's stage, speaking out about social inequality at a forum in Spain.

Her place in history, through marriage and widowhood, is likely to impress even her lifelong admirers. Most importantly, her work is not finished.

MOOR THOUGHTS ABOUT GRAÇA MACHEL

Those who know me well, know that the woman I most hope to meet in my world travels promoting a positive path through widowhood is Graça Machel. I've long been a loyal fan and admirer of her irrepressible spirit, her strong inner light that radiates around the world.

At Modern Widows Club HQ, they've heard me quote Graça many times. My latest favorite quote is: "We are all drops of water in the wave of change." A wave meant to inspire others to understand their own power, to discover their own irrepressible spirit. In fact, recently my staff sent me a notebook that sits on my desk emblazoned with this empowering quote burned into the cork cover. I cherish it.

In 2021, I was honored to be included on a human rights forum call with Graça as part of the United Nations Commission on the Status of Women webinar. That was the closest I've been in her presence, and even that was enough to encourage, to inspire me to strive for new heights of advocacy for the voiceless.

Losing one husband, as we all know too well, is heartbreaking almost beyond description. So the thought of losing two husbands in a lifetime, as Graça did, is simply inconceivable. When I feel low, I remember that Graça endured twice the heartbreak—once when a tragic plane crash took the life of Samora Machel, her husband of eleven years, then once again when she lost Nelson Mandela, who endured twenty-seven years of imprisonment before meeting and falling in love with her. Internalizing her strength and tenacity keeps me pressing on.

Certainly, as a first lady—twice—she was often a part of her husbands' conversations concerning global issues. Knowing her commitment to the health and welfare of women and children—a commitment I share with her—I can't help but imagine that she has deep dreams about finding solutions for these causes, solutions she can't communicate since they don't yet have an established worldwide language, solutions that she might discover in the space where the heart and head meet.

It empowers me to believe, as I imagine Graça does, that we all have a connection to divine appointments and happenings that occur in our lives, that we walk toward the uncertain and the unknown awaiting a message for the next step to appear. Walking in faith, not by sight. Knowing our own light is needed in any hero's journey, needed to illuminate a path no one may have walked before.

It gives me strength that she specifically focuses on causes supporting the lives of women and girls. She is my role model for people who can become leaders due to extraordinary circumstances. I understand that path, leading the charge for widow advocacy and awareness. Graça inspires me most with her lifetime of unselfishness, acting as a warrior for social justice for the underprivileged people of her homeland, her continent, and the world.

Graça has created a broad legacy for herself and her causes even while she carries the legacy of two great men and their causes. She is a source of eternal light for many women and widows. Indeed, Graça remains a distinguished woman and modern widow, staying active as a high-level advisor for the

Every Woman Every Child mobilization movement to address major health challenges faced by women, children, and adolescents around the world, as well as for The Elders global leadership group child marriage initiative Girls Not Brides: The Global Partnership to End Child Marriage.

When I do finally meet her, I will share the need for her advocacy for young widows in impoverished nations—where the average age of widowhood is thirty-nine—and how Modern Widows Club can bring inspiration and support and community to those women. I want her to know that many of the child brides she fights for will become child widows (a result of arranged marriages to elderly men), and sadly join the least visible and among the most forgotten widowhood demographics around the world.

It is largely because of Graça that I strive to revolutionize how widows are served and supported worldwide. Why I fight to be a revolutionary leader of significance. Graça has lit the way for me, inspiring me to work at building seemingly impossible pathways to acknowledgment and justice.

Her openness at admitting both her strengths and weaknesses is a quality I greatly admire. We can't do everything, but we can do the one thing that is possible right in front of us. Putting one foot in front of the other is a mantra I know we both respect and adhere to. It is a key component to a vibrant widowhood.

How deeply grateful I am to praise and promote her seventy-seven years of lighting the world with hope, holding the torch high so that others might experience human freedom for themselves.

QUESTIONS TO CONSIDER

Graça promotes women's and girls' causes because she believes in them herself. Do you have a personal experience that propels you to rally for a cause?

Have you ever received a scholarship to a course, program, workshop or event that changed your life's trajectory?

What does "bloom like a flower" mean to you?

8

TE ATA THOMPSON FISHER

Finding Her True Voice in Chickasaw Myth

Mary Frances Thompson Fisher—best known as Te Ata—was born a citizen of the Chickasaw Nation in the state of Oklahoma and became a performer of Native American stories. Her Chickasaw name means "Bearer of the Morning." In a career spanning more than sixty years, she shared Chickasaw legends, myths, and chants and performed rituals in her native regalia for audiences of all ages, preserving, promoting, and demonstrating great affection for the old ways, for Native Americans, and for natural beauty.

She was born in Emet, Chickasaw Nation, on December 3, 1895. Her parents were members of the Nation, with her father acting as its last treasurer, and her uncle, Douglas H. Johnston, the Nation's last governor. Johnston County, where Mary grew up, was named after her uncle at Oklahoma's statehood ceremony in 1907.

Mary went to elementary school at Bloomfield Academy in Johnston County. Later, she attended high school in Tishomingo, the county seat. She matriculated at Oklahoma College for Women (now the University of Science and Arts of Oklahoma), in Chickasha, where Francis Densmore Davis, an active researcher and writer on Native American culture, became her mentor. Davis recognized young Mary's talent for drama and encouraged her to embrace it. Soon, Mary began to use the name Te Ata, reflecting her native heritage.

In 1919, after she graduated college, Te Ata worked for a Chautauqua tent show circuit managed out of St. Louis, Missouri. She began to develop her style of storytelling using various Native American sources. Her readings, storytelling, and dances were often accompanied by classical and other music played on piano. Eventually, she also used small drums, rattles, and other common, traditional instruments. Te Ata said she wanted to share with others the richness, wisdom, and wonder of her Native American heritage.

She attended the Carnegie Institute of Technology in Pittsburgh, Pennsylvania, for one year. From Pittsburgh she moved to New York City, worked in theater, and entertained the city's social elite. There, Te Ata met George Clyde Fisher, a naturalist and eventual curator of the Hayden Planetarium. They married in 1933 and were together for sixteen years, until Fisher's death in 1949 at age seventy.

In 1933, United States President Franklin Roosevelt presented a performance by Te Ata at his first state dinner. Though many of her performances throughout the 1930s were given at summer camps in New England and New York State, in 1939, she performed for President Roosevelt again, this time at his home in Hyde Park, New York, on the occasion of a state visit by the king and queen of Great Britain.

Later, she toured Europe, performing for royal families and heads of state. The Fishers traveled in South America and extensively in the United States, often observing Native Indian ceremonies and learning different traditions. Te Ata incorporated these experiences into her performances and later in her storytelling.

Te Ata was fifty-six when her husband died. Early in her widowhood, she traveled and visited friends, but eventually came back to performing. She returned to Oklahoma in 1966. During the 1960s and '70s, activism among Native Americans started to show results, improving self-government, health care, and education for the Chickasaw people and other tribes. Te Ata was pleased, but continued to dramatize folklore and present the beauty and wisdom of Native American culture, educating all who came to see her perform.

In 1958, she was recognized by the Oklahoma Hall of Fame, and in 1976 she received the Oklahoma Governor's Award and was named Woman of the Year by *The Ladies Home Journal*. Her performances are preserved in a film, *God's Drum* (circa 1971), and on a video recording of a storytelling festival sponsored by the Oklahoma City Arts Council.

She died at age ninety-nine in Oklahoma City on October 26, 1995.

Te Ata Fisher's influence on the world's understanding and appreciation of Native American traditions and on the art of storytelling is an enduring legacy that remains powerful to this day.

MOOR THOUGHTS ABOUT TE ATA THOMPSON FISHER

When I first discovered Te Ata, I was immediately drawn to the light of her strong spirit. After her husband's death, sharing her Chickasaw heritage and Native American culture somehow made her inner light shine even brighter, helped her find and hold on to who she was in her heart and soul. Hers was an example of the kind of widowhood I wished to feel and exemplify in my own heart and soul.

Te Ata knew who she was from the time of her youth, through her marriage to Clyde Fisher, and then through her widowhood. Her sense of self never wavered. As she stepped out into the wide world, she was never far from the girl who grew up in Chickasaw Nation. Her Native American roots were her foundation for nearly one hundred years. I admire that kind of authenticity, that strength of character. I think it's an important part of letting the power of your light shine through. I strive to be as true to myself as Te Ata was to herself.

Learning about her life of adventures brought back memories of my own adventures. I was a young girl, born and living in the big City of Angels in California, and then suddenly my home was a small rural town in Arkansas, a new world of adventure for me. I was free to roam in the woods, to play with frogs, butterflies, lizards, stray cats, and insects. I fell in love with nature, with its ever-changing beauty. I like to think Te Ata felt this way about her journey as well.

Of course, she went on many wondrous adventures throughout her life and embraced each one with a leap of faith built on her Chickasaw foundation. I think there was a kind of peace inside of her—because of that foundation—that made it possible for her to carry on, to keep going. She wasn't just a performer, she was a profound storyteller bridging different cultures, an educator gracefully imparting nature's awesome lessons, the first of which may have been that accepting the beautiful differences in people is the true path to living peacefully as one nation…and to living peacefully within yourself.

I remember my mother talking about her grandmother who had a Native American background. My mother always spoke of her with awe and reverence, so I grew up with that sense of reverence as well. Looking inward now, it was a reverence for people who were different but similar at heart, all of them an important part of my sense of community. These generational family stories became the thread of my broader story of my life. The whole became greater than the sum of its parts. I think this was part of what Te Ata was teaching. It's a life lesson she reminded me of.

Te Ata inspired me to keep beating my own drum, to find the courage to advocate for issues I deeply cared about. I learned from her that no matter where I go in life, no matter what happens to me on my journey through widowhood, I must share my wisdom and shine the internal torch that lives within me to help light the way for others. To do this, I must keep my child's heart and voice alive and remain true to my foundation.

I hope you will keep Te Ata close to your heart while curating your own story of legacy. We can illuminate our past, present, and future dreams while honoring our humble and sacred beginnings that set the trajectory for our audacious futures. Yes, we can. Te Ata shows us how.

QUESTIONS TO CONSIDER

What myths are you living that are calling to you to find your true voice?

How is the story of your life that you tell to yourself and to others different than before?

Are you aware of your sacred story and how it impacts those around you in a profound and audacious way that is fulfilling for you?

OSA JOHNSON

I Married Adventure

In the small town of Chanute, Kansas, a story began in 1894 that reached around the world. Osa Leighty was the daughter of a Santa Fe railroad engineer. Though as a child she lived a simple life with her father, mother, grandmother, and younger brother, she became a pioneering photographer, filmmaker, author, and adventurer the likes of which had never been seen in Kansas or anywhere else.

At the age of six, Osa already distinguished herself as strong-willed and steadfast when she set her heart on having a traveling photographer take a picture of her three-year-old brother, Vaughn, dressed in his Sunday best. Vaughn, however, would not pose quietly—or for free, demanding the daunting sum of ten cents to sit still. After an exhausting battle of wills, Osa paid her brother the ten cents in a huff. The photographer, a teenage boy named Martin Johnson from the bigger city of Independence, Kansas, proved to be skilled at photographing little boys, and though neither knew it at the time, eight years later, Osa would meet him again.

She had a quiet upbringing in Chanute. Life was simpler at the turn of the century. Baking bread, gardening, and spending time with family and friends defined her life until the age of sixteen, when her best friend, Gail, quit school to become a singer. Osa spent Saturday afternoons applauding delightedly as Gail sang along to a slideshow at a motion picture theater. The girls had grown up dressing alike and were closer than sisters. When Gail abruptly married her long-time beau, Osa was crushed that their dreams of a double wedding were over. But she soon recovered from her hurt, boarded a train to visit her newlywed friend, and was surprised to again find herself in the company of her brother's photographer, Martin Johnson, who was now lecturing at the same theater where Gail performed, following her shows.

Though it wasn't love at first sight, Martin's charm and good nature quickly swept Osa off her feet. They were married by a judge, and then quickly married again in Missouri, since Osa was only sixteen. It was then, in their new apartment back in Independence, that they realized they had very different expectations for the future.

Martin was an adventurer at heart, having traveled around the world for two years with Jack London in a forty-five-foot boat christened the *Snark*. Osa soon became convinced to join her husband on his adventures. Before long, she was crucial to the success of their journeys.

Together, in 1917, they were the first photographers to document the Cannibals of the South Seas. She and Martin wrote about their adventures in Borneo, and created a film in 1918, when she was likely the first white woman who had visited the area.

During these years, they sailed on cramped boats, with fragile cameras and film that would not perform in heat and humidity. Osa served as planner and organizer for expeditions that would soon include dozens of people, who all needed to be fed. She arranged for food, medical supplies, cooking equipment, and staff who would live with them for weeks in remote areas. Using kerosene as insect repellent on her face, she cooked outdoors and slept in tents during downpours. They were able to survive in large part due to her skills at fishing and gardening.

After months of hardships, Osa and Martin returned to the United States to develop the film so they could present lectures across the country about the pygmies, cannibals, and other indigenous peoples they had encountered.

The young adventurers were firmly against hunting animals for sport and often tangled with wealthy Americans and others who were collecting "trophies." Their photographs and films told the stories of beautiful, graceful, majestic animals, especially elephants and lions.

However, the jungle was a dangerous place, and their beloved animals were fierce and unpredictable, so Osa learned to shoot several kinds of guns, saving her husband's life, and the lives of others, many times.

"My wife holds the gun," Martin said. "Thank Heaven I have found the right sort of woman to take along with me into the desert and the jungle. If ever a man needed a partner in his chosen vocation it has been I. And if ever a wife were a partner to a man, it is Osa Johnson."

Between expeditions, Osa and Martin spent weeks and months meeting with business backers like George Eastman of Eastman Kodak. They socialized with Will Rogers and other celebrities, such as Charlie Chaplin and, later, even with royalty.

Their lives swung from trading tobacco and beads in remote Africa to negotiating large investments on Wall Street. Osa knew she was an important part of the success of the expeditions, as well as Martin's happiness and health.

Their fellow adventurers questioned Martin for having a woman travel the dangerous world with him, but Osa knew that Martin's faith in her never wavered. He knew he would not have had such success without her. For him, she was the right combination of sweet and outdoorsy, his "good sport." Indeed, she was all of that and more from her teenage years to their last trip in 1937.

Throughout their many years of adventure on boats and in safari camps in jungles around the world, they had lost friends to disease and injury. They were away from their families during their entire marriage and missed being at the bedsides of their parents when they died. They carried their grief along with their excitement to the continents they explored.

And then, while in the United States for a lecture tour, on January 12, 1937, after a stop in Las Vegas, Nevada, their commercial Western Air Express Flight 7 (a Boeing 247D airliner) shockingly crashed at Los Pinetos Peak, outside of Burbank, California. Eleven people were injured.

Osa survived. But Martin did not recover.

I Married Adventure: The Lives and Adventures of Martin and Osa Johnson is her bestselling memoir. It was published in 1940, a tribute to her husband, with extensive details about their travels. Osa Johnson fought traditionalists to have her name appear as the author of her own memoir, as opposed to being recognized as Mrs. Martin Johnson. It was well before the time that society accepted a woman as independent of her husband. But Osa used her strength of will and her powerful light to push the envelope.

Osa and Martin are considered pioneers in the film industry, beginning in black-and-white silent films and continuing to color with sound. They began in 1912 with *Cannibals of the South Seas*. In widowhood, she wrote additional books about her life and adventures and produced and directed the film *Stanley and Livingstone* (1939) and the film *I Married Adventure* (1940).

With her husband, she authored twenty books, published more than one hundred articles, and brought the stories of Africa to mass audiences around the world.

She was described as beautiful, photogenic, charming, and a

crack shot who enjoyed high adventure. She had no equal when it came to tracking wildlife and organizing complex safaris.

Yet she was no tomboy. Her elegant wardrobe and great stage presence earned her the title of one of the best dressed women in America, introducing khaki safari wear that is still popular today.

Today both Martin and Osa are honored throughout Kansas as representing the best of Kansans. Osa's mother created the Martin and Osa Johnson Safari Museum in Chanute, where visitors can learn more about their daring adventures and enjoy the films in a restored Santa Fe railroad depot, which perfectly represents that remarkable time.

Osa continued to write books and produce films until her death from heart disease in January of 1953. She was the first person to produce a wildlife series on television. Her *Big Game Hunt* premiered eleven years before the more familiar *Mutual of Omaha's Wild Kingdom*.

She also designed jungle-themed jewelry and a cutting-edge sports fashion line called Osafari after long years of learning which clothing worked best in the rugged outdoors.

The popular movie and characters from Disney's *The Lion King* are inspired by wild animals from Osa and Martin's explorations. To this day, the Jambo House at Disney's Animal Kingdom's Lodge pays tribute to Martin and Osa Johnson within their Sunset Overlook Lounge, designed to transport guests to an African safari, respecting both nature and human cultures. The space features genuine safari objects, including period teacups, hats, binoculars, African artwork, diary pages, and a first-issue *I Married Adventure* book. Visitors can see an ongoing exhibit of photos from Osa and Martin's African expeditions. Only the exhibit in the Chanute museum is larger.

When the concept for Disney's Animal Kingdom Lodge was in its early stages (1997 and 1998), the Disney architects and designers borrowed films from the Martin and Osa Johnson Safari Museum in Chanute to better understand Africa's natural landscapes, wildlife, and safari life. Martin and Osa provided the Disney team (and its millions of visitors to this day) a unique lens into the Africa of the past.

What Osa Johnson created with her husband—and in her brilliant widowhood—powered by her indefatigable spirit and dogged inner light, made history that lives and shines as bright today as ever.

MOOR THOUGHTS ABOUT OSA JOHNSON

I'm inspired by Osa Johnson's small-town-girl-makes-it-big-in-the-world story because, like so many other women, I know what it's like to grow up in a small, rural town and dream about going on great adventures. I was always that girl looking for something *more*. Of course, I found just that when I met my late husband, Chad *Moor*, at an architectural workshop in Kansas. I'd traveled there to learn how to draw three-dimensional perspectives, and Chad was the guest speaker from Florida.

Osa also embarked on a mission of discovery. She traveled to support her girlfriend in a theater production only to find her future husband, Martin Johnson.

Like Osa, I grew up a bona fide tomboy, unafraid to venture into places that were untraditionally specific for the girls at the time. Like Osa, I learned that not abiding by societal rules presented life experiences that otherwise wouldn't have happened.

Osa embodied a kind of confidence that was unusual for a young woman whose life experience was limited to a rural setting. But she was a big dreamer and believed that marrying Martin would be an adventure—being by his side as his wife and partner, breaking societal rules together, would present her, and them, the exciting experiences she'd always dreamed of.

She was right. She fell in love with a filmmaker and photographer explorer and journeyed with him around the world, traversing jungles, photographing wildlife and indigenous peoples, dreaming big and then making those dreams happen.

What she learned was that no dream is too big, no journey impossible, no adventure unworthy of exploration. With her husband, she discovered what true partnership meant, that strength from both sides maximizes impact and legacy, joy and love.

These were lessons that would later help her in widowhood. And through the power of her inner light, they were lessons that would help me through mine.

It was in my widowhood that I discovered Osa in a small museum in the Disney's Animal Kingdom Lodge in Orlando, Florida, called the Sunset Lounge. The museum highlights Osa and Martin's work with wildlife and influence on deep jungle safaris. I was drawn to her strength and courage and a few years later traveled to Chanute, Kansas, to learn more about her enduring spirit at the Martin and Osa Johnson Safari Museum. I even met with the museum curator to get a greater sense of Osa's legacy.

She was the wife and partner and woman who held the rifle, protecting her husband as he filmed in the deepest jungles, wild animals all around them. She was the wife and partner and woman who organized and managed their worldwide travels, safaris into uncharted territories, calculating the cost of supplies and manpower, doing the job of a CEO, COO, and CFO with ease and grace before it was accepted practice for a woman to wield this kind of power.

She earned respect quietly while she was married, and then demanded it after she was widowed, fighting publishing traditionalists to have her name listed as the author of *I Married Adventure*, as opposed to being told she must be credited as Mrs.

Martin Johnson. She insisted she be credited as Osa Johnson. Her light and faith as a married woman was strong but stronger still as a widow.

By the example of her life, Osa taught me to earn respect by immersing myself in the experiences of my life. By being alive and involved. By standing up for what's right and then by lighting the path for those who follow. Finding herself in the spotlight as a widow, she never wavered in continuing to share the journeys and adventures she and her husband embarked on, the wonders they discovered, the glory and majesty of the animals, the dignity of the native peoples, the light of sunsets and sunrises on the savannah, the flickering light projected in the films they shared with fascinated viewers.

Living her life in the wild, far from her humble beginnings, she found a world of possibility, a lifetime of passion that still influences generations of women and widows. I am one of those widows who have looked to her light, who have taken on her legacy and opened myself to any opportunity to step into the wild, which, for most of us, means to step outside our comfort zones.

For me, Osa is a role model for the ages, a woman to look up to, and a widow to be inspired by. Her influence, her legacy, her light, remains relevant and strong and bright.

QUESTIONS TO CONSIDER

Osa felt her life took her on an adventure from the moment she partnered with Martin and that feeling continued into her widowhood. Do you feel the sense of adventure in your relationship, past and present? Do you have a bucket list of places you'd like to travel to?

Have you felt that your upbringing prepared you well for the stage of many shifts and pivots in widowhood?

Could you move to a faraway place and start a whole new life exploring new possibilities?

VEUVE CLICQUOT

La Grande Dame of Champagne

Born in 1777, in Reims, France, Barbe-Nicole Ponsardin was eleven years old when the French Revolution began. The eldest daughter of a wealthy businessman, she was suddenly in danger. The streets of Reims were crowded with angry mobs calling for equality and freedom. As a member of the social elite, the small, serious girl was disguised and shepherded through the crowd by her dressmaker.

Her grandfather employed nearly one thousand people in his textile factories. At the time, the manufacture of soft woolen goods was the primary business in the region (long before the appearance of Champagne's famous sparkling wines, including and especially the one named for Barbe-Nicole—"Veuve Clicquot," which is translated as Widow Clicquot).

But Barbe-Nicole was not interested in textiles or fashions. Her sister, Clémentine, was the willowy, pretty daughter whose elegant portrait still remains part of the family history. Very few documents or photographs of Barbe-Nicole survived the centuries, though it's possible to imagine what her life was like.

Married at age twenty-one to the dashing François Clicquot, son of a wealthy merchant, the arrangement was not one of love or hope but was to benefit both families. The practice of religion had ended officially in France in 1794, making a church wedding illegal. The young couple dressed simply and were quietly married in the cellars beneath her family's grand estate. These interconnected cellars had been left behind by Roman quarry workers and were often used as storage and even wine cellars.

The two had probably known each other for years as their families were in the same business. The Clicquot family additionally operated as wine brokers, and perhaps even sold wine to the Ponsardins to celebrate the birth of Barbe-Nicole all those years earlier.

François had been educated abroad, and escaped the draft while in Switzerland. His family, like hers, had put on a show of patriotism, but had so far escaped the military and the rigors of war. Instead, he worked in commercial import and export administration as part of his military duty, still on French soil.

They married upon his return to Reims, and the two of them began to manage their extensive vineyards. François dreamed of exporting wine to Europe, and shared these ambitions with his wife. Because he clashed with his father, he brought her into the discussions much more frequently than might the typical husband and businessman of the day.

At this time in history, though women were becoming more likely to run small family businesses such as dressmaking, they remained invisible in larger companies. As a traveling salesman for the company, François was away from home for months at a time, and Barbe-Nicole stepped into the day-to-day operations. François had early success in 1804, in the foreign markets, but war and weather drained their capital. Exhausted and disappointed with his business failure, François contracted a fever and battled with typhoid for two weeks.

It was then, at age twenty-seven, Barbe-Nicole buried her husband, leaving her a solo parent to their six-year-old daughter, Clémentine.

Fighting rumors that François had been profoundly depressed and had taken his own life, Barbe-Nicole was suddenly in conversations with her father-in-law about the family business. He was ready to liquidate, unable to imagine a future without his son.

But she had come from a family of entrepreneurs and surely knew of the Widow Robert or the Widow Blanc, both of whom had inherited wine businesses a generation earlier. However, these women were not from the genteel class, not from the drawing rooms and dinner parties that Barbe-Nicole had grown up in. Her other role model was her sister, who was a fashionable lady of leisure.

Her family probably would have wanted her to remarry to ease her grief, to provide a father for her daughter. Instead, she took advantage of her role as a widow in that era of French culture, in which she was allowed many social and financial freedoms. Married women had restrictions placed on their lives, especially in business, that no longer applied to her. Even in the middle of another war, she resolved to dress in black and continue to operate her family business—with a new business partner.

Her lifestyle and culture also allowed her to send her young daughter away to Paris for school. With cousins there to look out for her, young Clémentine would learn needlework and other arts in addition to reading and writing. This set the stage for Barbe-Nicole to become a working mother leading the family wine business.

Her day would have begun early, with account books and correspondence, before traveling to her vineyards and wine cellars. Shortly after she and François had married, and long before the use of wine labels and logos became a common business practice, the family began using an anchor as a company symbol. The traditional symbol of hope, it may have also reminded her of the exports and ocean trade that François had initiated.

When her contract with her business partner ended after their initial four-year agreement, Barbe-Nicole was cash-strapped. Waiting for a grape harvest or for wine to age were business realities not helping to pay her workers. While her salesman was traveling for wine orders, she had him sell some of her family jewelry to pay her bills.

The harvest of 1811 produced outstanding grapes. This was the year a comet passed through the northern hemisphere, drawing all eyes to the night sky, and the world was filled with hope for the future.

However, the harvest was simply the first step. The market softened with the abundance. Some of the wine was in barrels and could be sold quickly, but the aging process for sparkling wines could take two years. During that time, the economy and the war blockades continued and grew worse. With a Russian invasion approaching, Barbe-Nicole closed up her cellars to protect her inventory. But when they arrived, the Russians did not destroy her wine. Instead, they enjoyed it and even became customers when they returned home.

This vintage, finally, brought success internationally. With a comet emblazoned on the cork, it was sold throughout Europe. Her salesman, Luis Bohne, wrote to her: *Delicious to taste, it is an assassin, and anyone who wants to make its acquaintance will become well attached to his chair, because after paying his respects to a bottle, he will go looking for crumbs under the tables.*

The science of winemaking, her ingenuity, and her perseverance combined to make her a celebrity, even with competitors such as Dom Perignon and Moët & Chandon. Barbe-Nicole was not just the first woman to build a commercial champagne company, she was one of only a handful of entrepreneurs to succeed. She had a gift for business. She could have simply managed her husband's business, as other widows did in her era, but instead she modernized the industry, made a vast fortune, and expanded a company that remains at the top of its industry.

Tilar J. Mazzeo's biography, *The Widow Clicquot*, also details Barbe-Nicole's innovations in manufacturing, glass production for bottles, the mushroom shaped champagne cork and even the shape of the wine glasses used for champagne.

Barbe-Nicole's daughter was pursued by wealthy and prominent men and chose Count Louis Marie Joseph of Chevigné for marriage. A difficult personality with expensive habits, Louis was nevertheless charming, and Barbe-Nicole indulged his needs for larger and larger houses. Soon a granddaughter vied for her attention, and Barbe-Nicole began to consider who would take over her business. She began working more closely with one of her employees, got back into textiles, and even opened a bank. Both businesses were unsuccessful. It is thought that she may have been suffering from grief after the death of her father in 1820, feeling a loss of hope after so many successes.

Barbe-Nicole's lifetime of hard work and success ensured that her family would have the luxuries she desired for them. Though the first celebrity businesswoman remained a workaholic, she started to spend more time at her country estates. She began to enjoy her time as a grandmother, and to pull back from her daily work schedule.

Barbe-Nicole died in 1866, at the age of eighty-nine. Her childhood expectations of a quiet life and likely future of family dinner parties had ended before they began, when she became the Widow Clicquot. Few people have seen her picture or know her story, but her name became synonymous with luxury, celebration, and champagne toasts.

MOOR THOUGHTS ABOUT VEUVE CLICQUOT

I feel a close connection to Barbe-Nicole, better known as Veuve Clicquot (Widow Clicquot). I consider her to be among the first women I thought of as a modern widow, a trailblazer who forged her path after the death of her husband with a powerful light that has inspired me throughout my journey through widowhood.

Barbe-Nicole was married for seven short years, knowing her husband only a few years before taking the next step toward building a life together. I was also married for seven (too-short) years, knowing my husband and partner only a few years before deciding to marry. Like Barbe-Nicole, who worked beside her husband in their vineyards and offices, I also worked alongside my husband in our office. My marriage was the joining of two consenting, independent adults who found each other by happenstance, fell in love, and mutually consented to be partners in life. By contrast, Barbe-Nicole's marriage was arranged, a business transaction to satisfy the two families involved. Still, when my husband died, I had to speak with my father-in-law to resolve business matters involving my deceased spouse, his late son, just as Barbe-Nicole had to meet with her father-in-law. Like her, I did not always see eye-to-eye with my husband's father.

But also like Barbe-Nicole and her husband's father, we were all trying to find a way through the hard loss we had suffered.

It's hard to imagine that arranged marriages to satisfy business concerns exist today, and yet they do for many women and girls around the world.

Together, my husband and I had built a fifty-person architectural and design firm. Though not an international wine and champagne company, I felt (and feel) a kinship with Barbe-Nicole as an entrepreneurial-minded woman battling to succeed against all odds.

In addition to grief and motherhood and business finances, Barbe-Nicole had to contend with war and religion and breaking the mold of the traditional roles women were supposed to stay within. For me—and for many modern widows—it was partners pushing me/buying me out of my business, struggling to care for two young daughters, and wondering how I would keep the cash coming in to pay the mortgage and buy food and clothes and so on...plus survive the debilitating impact of prolonged grief.

Yes, as a modern widow, I wasn't sure I could press on, asking myself, like Barbe-Nicole may have, why I had survived, not wanting to face my new unbelievable reality. Many modern widows face these moments. Hopefully, something clicks into place in the back of your mind, and you realize you survived for a reason, though that reason has yet to be revealed.

Such was the case for Barbe-Nicole, who realized safety and protection of her family was her reason for survival. The Widow Clicquot attracted predators, as I did, as many modern widows do. But she soon realized she had to stand up to them and learn who she could and couldn't trust in order to protect her family.

Barbe-Nicole's inspirational rallying cry moved me just when I needed it to. She was an out-of-the-box thinker, finding her courage, her inner strength, to forge her own path—a *new* path—and then shining her light on the path so others could follow. This is what makes her so very special in my eyes.

It's this idea of creating a *new* path for yourself that I think is the most inspirational part of Barbe-Nicole's story. Unexpected opportunities present themselves when you harness your courage and shine your light and set out to build a path for yourself. *Good things happen to good people doing brave things* is the inspiration I took from Barbe-Nicole. It's a terrific mantra for a modern widow.

If you must be different, then be different, but still be true to who you are. That's another inspirational life idea Barbe-Nicole taught me. She was different at a time when almost all aspects of a woman's life were predetermined for her.

But Barbe-Nicole parented differently, grandparented differently, and did business differently. No doubt everyone had an opinion as to what she should be doing with her life, her child, and her business. Plenty of modern widows, including me, know this experience all too well.

Barbe-Nicole proved them all wrong. She maneuvered her way through the science of making wine and champagne with an eye toward standing out, being different, being special. She designed the mushroom-shaped champagne cork we still use today. She tapped her courage and creativity and ingenuity to solve problems, to be among the first successful modern widows.

Her competitive spirit inspired me to nurture my own, to seek *new* widow solutions and support systems that didn't yet exist. By looking at the problems many widows face, hearing them voice their fears and concerns and dreams, I often ask myself how I can serve these special women differently and better for future generations.

Barbe-Nicole taught me—and teaches me still—that there is always a way forward if we embrace the changes that come from *new*. New places, people, situations, and ideas. That we as widows are a groundswell of bright ingenuity waiting to be toasted as the light of the party. Barbe-Nicole was a modern widow before there was such a thing as modern widows.

Not that widowhood is a party to be celebrated. Surely it is not. But living through our widowhood-survivor mission, building resilience and reaching back to help others thrive is a life goal worth achieving *and* toasting. Indeed, among the many accomplishments women have made in their widowhood, grief-to-growth stories have always been and will always be a reason to celebrate.

Like Widow Clicquot, who chose the anchor as her champagne's symbol, modern widows can bind themselves to their inner light and create life-worth-living moments worthy of celebration.

Cheers to that!

QUESTIONS TO CONSIDER

Veuve Clicquot inherited assets (family traditions, property, reputation) that she didn't know what to do with. Have you experienced the weight of that reality?

As a woman in society, has becoming a widow changed others' perspectives of you? In what way?

Do you feel you are a natural-born leader now in widowhood?

11

ELEANOR ROOSEVELT

Breaking the Mold at the White House

When United States President Franklin Roosevelt died, his wife, First Lady Eleanor, lost her husband, the father of her five children, her president, her home of twelve years, and her identity as First Lady. At age sixty-one, she endured the same issues that beset many widows. How she handled those challenges, how she went on to become what Harry Truman called "the First Lady of the World," is what makes her story so powerful.

Eleanor was born October 11, 1884, in New York City. Orphaned before she was ten years old, her mother died of diphtheria and her father from alcoholism. After their deaths, she was sent to live with her maternal grandmother in Tivoli in the Hudson Valley in New York. At age fifteen, her grandmother sent her to Allenswood Academy in London where she was influenced by a teacher, Marie Souvestre, who championed liberal causes and the study of history. Eleanor traveled with Souvestre, who exposed her to impoverished areas of Europe. Profoundly influenced by her teacher and travel experiences, when Eleanor returned to New York City she became involved in social projects such as the National Consumers League.

Franklin Delano Roosevelt was Eleanor's fifth cousin once removed. On a train trip to her grandmother's, Eleanor encountered Franklin on his way to Harvard, and their courtship began. They were married on March 17, 1905.

Franklin's mother, Sara, objected to the marriage because the couple was too young and Eleanor was not sufficiently prominent. After the marriage, Sara made many decisions for Eleanor and Franklin, including finding them an appropriate place to live—an adjoining townhouse with connecting doors. Within ten years of their marriage, Eleanor and Franklin had six children, one girl and five boys. One of the boys died as an infant.

In 1911, Franklin was elected to the New York Senate as a representative of Dutchess County, where he and his mother retained residency in Hyde Park, and the family moved to Albany. About starting their life anew, Eleanor said, "For the first time I was going to live on my own. I wanted to be independent. I was beginning to realize that something within me craved to be an individual."

In Albany, Eleanor learned about politics by watching her husband fight Tammany Hall, an American political organization that played a major role in controlling the votes of New York City and New York State officials.

When Franklin was appointed Assistant Secretary of the United States Navy in 1913, Eleanor aided her husband in his role as a Cabinet officer. But with the outbreak of World War I, Eleanor became active with the Navy-Marine Corps Relief Society and the American Red Cross and realized she could be active independent of her husband's career. She accepted more public invitations, including one to visit shell-shocked sailors at St. Elizabeth Hospital in Washington, D.C.

In 1913, Eleanor hired Lucy Mercer as her private secretary, and in 1918 discovered Franklin's affair with Lucy. The couple considered and rejected divorce. Franklin promised in 1918 that he would never see Lucy again.

In 1920, Franklin was nominated to be Vice President of the United States on the Democratic ticket, but the Republicans won the election, so the Roosevelts returned to New York City and Hyde Park. By this time, their relationship had become more of a professional collaboration than a traditional marriage, with each having their own social and political support. When Franklin was diagnosed with polio in 1921, Eleanor continued her political activism in part as a means of keeping Franklin interested in living.

When Franklin was elected President of the United States in 1932, Eleanor held a press conference. She would meet with women reporters once a week to make the public more aware of White House activities and to encourage a more transparent understanding of the political process. With the same goal in mind, Eleanor also accepted an offer to write a monthly column for *Woman's Home Companion*, donating her fee to charity. She wrote about her daily life in a syndicated column, "My Day," from 1935 until her death in 1962.

As the United States Great Depression deepened, Eleanor became aware of poor conditions in West Virginia. She fought for and promoted the Subsistence Homestead Division, a program that was part of the National Industrial Recovery Act.

In her second term as First Lady, Eleanor increased her civil rights activism by advocating anti-lynching legislation, abolishing the poll tax, and speaking in favor of National Sharecropper's Week.

During World War II, Eleanor worked to allow the immigration of refugee children into the United States and later said one of her greatest regrets in life was not doing enough to encourage Franklin to accept more refugees fleeing Nazism. She continued her activism on behalf of African Americans and New Deal domestic programs, traveled to England and the South Pacific to boost morale among soldiers, and co-chaired the newly-formed United States Office of Civilian Defense.

On April 12, 1945, Franklin was at the Little White House in Warm Springs, Georgia. Eleanor was in Washington, D.C., attending a musical program at the Seagrave Club. The First Lady was summoned to a telephone and was told Franklin had died.

She quickly went to Warm Springs, where Franklin's cousin, Laura Delano, revealed that Lucy Mercer Rutherfurd had been with Franklin for three days before his death. Eleanor learned that Franklin had seen Lucy often, particularly during the war years and after Lucy's husband, Paul Rutherfurd, died in 1944. Eleanor also discovered that her own daughter, Anna, had facilitated the visits between her father and Lucy.

In addition to the turmoil of this betrayal, Eleanor had to deal with complications such as the inability to find Franklin's plan for his funeral and the timing of the funeral due to the Germans and Japanese taking advantage of the transition by Harry S. Truman from Vice President to President.

On the train ride back to Washington from Georgia, Eleanor made three decisions, as later detailed in her 1958 book, *On My Own*. She did not want to run a complex household again, she did not want to stop being useful, and she did not want to feel old.

In another of her authored books, *You Learn by Living*, Eleanor recalled in 1960 that she faced the challenges of early widowhood by repeating these words: *You must do the thing you think you cannot do.*

After twelve years of White House residency, Eleanor and the staff packed quickly, and on her last night there, she wrote to a friend, "I have a great sense of relief." She was pleased she would no longer be limited by what was thought appropriate for a first lady to say, advocate, or do. She said that writing "My Day" was more fun now that she was free to be more honest, more true about expressing her thoughts and feelings.

In response to a request for words of advice or comfort for a newly widowed woman from a reader of Eleanor's long-running advice column, "If You Ask Me," Eleanor encouraged her to stay very busy and to find interest in many things, and as many people, as she could. Being alone after the loss of a loved one was very difficult, she wrote, and she felt it was easier when one was occupied.

In 1945, Eleanor accepted President Harry Truman's appointment as the only female member of the United States delegation to the newly formed United Nations because she thought she might be able to use her experiences as a source of value to the nation and the world. She was not only advocating for Franklin's dream of lasting world peace through an international organization but was also making a statement for women to be involved in that pursuit as well. She saw that her presence at the United Nations was a model for women in a world where many millions of women could not vote or be involved in politics.

At the United Nations, Eleanor was assigned to the Social, Humanitarian, and Culture Committee, where she wrote and edited the Universal Declaration of Human Rights, the most enduring legacy of her time at the United Nations. In her later position as Human Rights Commission Chair, she presented the declaration on December 10, 1948, to the United Nations General Assembly, where it passed.

Throughout her life, Eleanor shined her light as an active member of the Democratic party. She advocated for civil rights as a board member of the National Association for the Advancement of Colored People and for labor rights, including equal pay for women. She continued her activism even during the last two years of her life, after being diagnosed with aplastic anemia and tuberculosis.

Eleanor passed away on November 7, 1962. A year later, the playwright and former Franklin D. Roosevelt speechwriter Archibald MacLeish wrote that only rarely does a great name become greater in death, as Eleanor's unquestionably had.

MOOR THOUGHTS ABOUT ELEANOR ROOSEVELT

Eleanor. A name that stands on its own, like Cher or Elvis or Oprah, but in a completely different super-stardom way. Eleanor. Once called "The First Lady of the World," that moniker still rings true today. Eleanor. A woman of humble beginnings who forged a reputation of worldwide acclaim and substance before women could do such things. Eleanor.

This woman and widow has always been a giant in my mind and heart, so much so that I've found it difficult to express the magnitude of soaring admiration I feel for her. Her renown grew far and wide at a time in history when global fame and impact were not fueled by instant social media, which, of course, did not exist in her lifetime. But neither was the media of her era responsible for her larger-than-life impact on the world she lived in. It was all her. Her words, her actions, her love, her light. It was Eleanor's personal connection with the people she touched that left an enduring memory on them…and on us.

From her orphaned beginnings to serving as the First Lady of the United States, she left a century of social impact the world had never seen before. As the first Chair of the United Nations Commission on the Status of Women (CSW), formed in 1945, she became a voice for women in the workplace, advocating that women's rights be considered in any crafting of national policy.

The CSW is an annual conference I attend to better understand and support women's struggles and the solutions needed to make change, specifically to ensure widows are heard. I'm grateful that for the first time in history, in 2022, widows were included as a topic of focus post the COVID-19 pandemic.

Though, as Eleanor likely did, I wonder why it takes so long.

I continue to honor Eleanor's legacy of standing up for human rights by picking up the torch she lit so long ago, ensuring the fourteen to fifteen million modern American widows of today have a voice in political forums. I channel Eleanor's strength and light, believing she would have been involved in this mission as well, tapping her own widowhood experience and the widowhood experiences of her mother-in-law, who guided her during the years as First Lady of the United States.

Eleanor knew that public health for women needed to be prioritized after being named first chair of the United Nations Commission on Human Rights. Long before it was common practice, she believed that protecting widows' rights was equal to protecting women's rights—which was the same as protecting human rights. That in order to find peace and equality in a world that often forgets them, women need to be valued.

One of my widow mentors, Margaret Owen, a human rights attorney and founder of Widows for Peace Through Democracy, once said "There is no peace until widows find peace." A statement that is both profound and true. So profoundly true, in fact, that I have devoted my working life to helping widows find peace.

In order for there to ever be a resolution to the most challenging issues of our time, the issues widows face will concurrently need to be addressed. For me, this is the last great social cause of significance.

I feel sure that were she alive today, Eleanor, shining her

empowering light, would be fighting this fight as well. Indeed, she inspires me to continue the march for justice and health equity for all women, especially widows. Especially fatherless daughters, the next generation of potential widows themselves. With Eleanor as inspiration, we can educate and build a better bridge of knowledge, support, and solutions for the new generations of widows to come.

Eleanor was a woman who would accept no boundaries. When barriers existed, she would challenge them, presenting her deep personal convictions of what life was meant to be. Her quiet determination was unstoppable. Her grit and grace in the toughest of times are qualities I strive to emulate.

Coincidentally, we share the same zodiac sign. Aquarius. Zodiac fans may recognize the character traits in our First Lady of the World. Quintessentially humanitarian. Boundlessly energetic. The willingness to play hardball when there's no other way to support those in need of strength and dignity. Organized with an extraordinary ability to stick to a strategy. A remarkable ability to learn from mistakes, make corrections, and march on. As a fellow Aquarian, these are the traits I strive for in my work in support of modern widows. Eleanor, no surprise, is my inspiration. If I'd had the honor of meeting her, I imagine I might have been immediately comfortable as her *wister* (widow + sister).

When I was interviewed by (another Aquarian) Oprah in 2006 as a formidable though unknown young widowed mother who had chosen to live an empowered life, overcoming great adversity as a solo parent, Oprah called me a hero that no one knew. That moment, that statement, caused me to take another look at myself and wonder if she could be right about me? Logging into the strength and inspiration I draw from Eleanor and other legendary widows, I now know she was.

I have learned that there exists an ethereal ease when one feels connected to another who is soulfully aligned with them. A visionary dreamer who shares the dream. We, all of us, modern widows especially, must welcome the rays of light shared in our direction. We must let them guide us back to who we truly are. We must allow them to make us feel at home.

Eleanor sent rays of light to women and widows and all unsupported people of the world. She made others feel at home simply by being near her. In her unique and powerful way, she was a radical way maker and healer—seeing, hearing, caring about, and fighting for the dignity of all humans became her life's work.

Eleanor was a woman and widow who changed history and *herstory*. Her name and legacy grew with her, at first beyond the death of her husband and then beyond her own death. Individualism paired with compassion and empathy was her greatest attribute, the power behind her inner light. She was a blessing to humanity, keeping our hearts warm even in the coldest of modern realities. Inspiring us to see that no one is truly orphaned if they find and become part of a community that cares.

QUESTIONS TO CONSIDER

Eleanor's experience as a young orphan who traveled to conflict areas of the world shaped her compassionate approach to others later in widowhood. Do you see the world more compassionately from your own experiences now?

When you see inequities in the world, are you comfortable stepping in and voicing your thoughts when issues arise?

Widowhood is the biggest transition in a woman's life. How many transitions have you known in the arc of womanhood?

12

BETTY FORD

Addressing Taboo Topics with Courage and Candor

Because of her candor and willingness to share her most personal and painful issues, Betty Ford, wife of United States President Gerald Ford, changed how people think of the First Lady.

Born in Chicago, Illinois, on April 8, 1918, Elizabeth Anne (Betty) Bloomer was raised in Grand Rapids, Michigan. Her father passed away, taking his own life, in 1934, when Betty was sixteen years old, leaving her mother a widow for fourteen years.

At a young age, Betty developed a passion for dance. She attended the Bennington School of Dance in Vermont, where she met choreographer Martha Graham. Betty followed Graham to New York City, where she became a member of Graham's dance troupe. Betty later wrote that more than anyone else, Graham shaped her life.

After New York, Betty returned to Grand Rapids, where she

taught dance to children with disabilities. In 1942, she married William Warren; they divorced five years later.

Soon, a friend introduced her to a local lawyer, Gerald Ford. The couple married on October 15, 1948, two weeks before Gerald was elected to his first term in Congress. Betty and Gerald moved to Washington, D.C., the nation's capital, where he served as a member of the United States House of Representatives for twenty-five years.

Betty spent much of her Washington time volunteering with the 81st Congress Club, the Congressional Wives Club, and the National Federation of Republican Women. She also provided tours of the Capitol to visiting constituents from Michigan.

Between 1950 and 1957, she and Gerald became parents of four children. Much of the childrearing responsibilities fell to Betty because Gerald was on the road campaigning.

In the mid-1960s, Betty developed a pinched nerve and spinal arthritis. Doctors prescribed pain medicine to which she became addicted—as she later admitted.

Her relatively unobtrusive role as the wife of a congressman expanded dramatically in October 1973 when United States Vice President Spiro Agnew resigned and President Richard Nixon named Gerald as Vice President. Betty understood that with Watergate still resonating across the country, Americans demanded more honesty from their public officials. Soon after moving into the White House, she held her first press conference.

Her commitment to openness was tested when, in 1974, just weeks after she moved into the White House, her doctors performed a mastectomy, removing her cancerous right breast. Previous first ladies had concealed their illnesses, but the Fords decided to disclose the facts.

Moved by her example, women coast to coast went to their physicians for breast examinations, and Betty recognized the enormous power a First Lady has to make a difference in the lives of American women and women around the world.

Using humor and straightforward honesty to express herself on controversial issues of the day, she answered questions about abortion rights, women in politics, and a proposed Equal Rights Amendment to the Constitution. On the widely watched CBS show *60 Minutes*, she openly shared her thoughts on such challenging issues as abortion rights, premarital sex, and marijuana use. Her forthright opinions drew criticism from some politicians, but her popularity soared and, in 1975, *Time* magazine named her one of the Women of the Year.

Betty was an enthusiastic supporter of her husband during the 1976 United States presidential election campaign. She participated in several speaking tours throughout the East and Midwest. Her popularity was proclaimed on lapel buttons that announced *Betty's Husband for President!* When Gerald Ford was defeated by former Georgia governor Jimmy Carter, the couple left Washington and moved to Rancho Mirage, California.

In California, Betty's dependence on prescription drugs continued. In early 1978, under pressure from her family, she agreed to enter a rehab center in Long Beach. In 1982, after her successful treatment there, the former First Lady co-founded the Betty Ford Center to help treat others suffering similar addictions and chaired the board of directors until 2005.

As a philanthropist, Betty worked relentlessly to help raise funds for the advancement of research and to design treatments to assist men, women, and families in recovery from alcoholism and other dependencies. The Betty Ford Center merged with the Hazelden Foundation in 2014 and remains one of the most outstanding rehab facilities in the world.

In facing her personal problems, Betty Ford dealt openly and honestly with the public. Her 1978 autobiography, *The Times of My Life*, chronicled her journey through the White House years and concluded with a candid, unplanned chapter on her admittance for rehab in Long Beach.

Her second book, *Betty: A Glad Awakening*, published in 1987, recounted her experience of recovery from chemical dependency.

She became an active and outspoken champion of improved awareness, education, and treatment for alcohol and drug dependencies.

In 1991 she was awarded a Presidential Medal of Freedom by United States President George H.W. Bush for her efforts to promote public awareness and treatment of alcohol and drug addiction. Betty and Gerald Ford received a Congressional Gold Medal in 1999.

After her husband's death on December 26, 2006, Betty, age eighty-eight, led her family and the nation with grace and strength through several days of national memorial observances.

Betty died on July 8, 2011 at the Eisenhower Medical Center in Rancho Mirage, California, at the age of ninety-three. After ceremonies in California and Michigan, she was interred beside her husband on the grounds of the Gerald R. Ford Presidential Museum in Grand Rapids.

To this day, Betty Ford is considered a pioneering first lady for her frank and honest handling of personal crises. From revealing her diagnosis of breast cancer to admitting her addiction to pain medication, Betty was a role model for recognizing and addressing problems. Her commitment to helping people recover from addiction continues to inspire that work today and is a legendary tribute to her memory.

MOOR THOUGHTS ABOUT BETTY FORD

At first glance, you might think Betty Ford was a "traditional" woman, and in some ways you'd be right. But there's no denying that during her life-journey she became a woman to be reckoned with, a woman who inspires me every day.

Betty learned early in her life that a woman can be independent if she chooses to. After her father died, she watched her mother venture into the real estate realm and thrive. It was an impressionable time for a young teenager, and Betty never forgot her mother's strong example.

Her early experience in dance became a passion that gave her a sense of control over both her body and her life. In the strongest sense, Betty found herself through dance. More importantly, the progressive dance environment introduced her to her muse and mentor, Martha Graham, a modern dance pioneer. Martha believed and taught that making your emotional self public through stage dancing was an empowering way to become the most authentic person you could be. This philosophy shaped Betty and became a theme for her life from that point forward.

Betty became a dancer and a dance instructor and was married young and then divorced young—her first marriage, which she chose to end, lasting five years. After that relationship was over, she was patient, waited another five years, taking time to heal before getting involved with someone again.

Then, when she was ready, she married Gerald Ford, a conservative lawyer who had political aspirations. Gerald brought stability to her life, and she brought independent energy to his. Theirs was an opposites-attract relationship—different strengths, different temperaments, different worldviews—that would serve them well later in the political realm, when Gerald was welcomed by both sides of the aisle in United States Congress. They were an affable, likable, and approachable couple.

Moving with her husband to Washington, D.C., into the swirling political whirlwind of the United States capital city, she became the quintessential, 1950s wife and mother, caring for her four children (born over seven years) while her husband served in Congress. And like many mothers, maybe especially in that era, she put her children and family first.

She began feeling less important with lower self-esteem and realized she was lonely without her husband, who traveled two hundred days a year. In retrospect, it was much like widowhood, where the absence of your life partner is acutely painful. But Betty wasn't widowed, she was simply solo parenting. Modern widows everywhere, me included, can relate to this part of Betty's story, the sacrifices and joys of being a dedicated but lonely mother.

By the 1960s, she was experiencing nerve pain and spinal arthritis from bearing and caring for so many small children in such a short span of time. The pain led to pain relievers. And the pain relievers led to an addiction. It was a tragic turn in her life, though completely understandable. All mothers, any mother, *me* as a widowed mother, would and will do anything to be well enough to care for our children. Betty was the same.

She was transparent about how the medications caused her addiction at a time when no one—especially not a wife and mother, and extra-especially not the wife of a well-known political figure—ever shared that kind of information publicly. She was also the first to speak about numbing her emotional pain with those prescribed medications. She talked about losing her identity and needing help. It was the '60s, and women had only just begun to openly express their deeper thoughts and feelings instead of keeping them buried inside, hidden away, like they'd done in the '50s. Betty was a plainspoken pioneer for the women's public platform.

Her behavior challenged the prevailing thought of that time, that fulfillment as a woman had only one definition: to be a housewife and a mother, that women who were truly feminine shouldn't *want* to work, get an education, or have political opinions. Standing up to this kind of closed-minded thinking prepared her for her future as a Vice President's wife in one of the most tumultuous times in American history.

If you're a woman—a widow—looking for inspiration, as I was, Betty challenging rooted and wrong-minded public opinion was a role model with whom I genuinely and wholeheartedly aligned. She intuitively knew that although she deeply loved her children and husband, she had the capacity to love in other equally empowering ways outside the home. I'm grateful for the path she forged for women today, again, me included, to have public convictions that go against the grain if need be.

Betty made up her own mind, formed her own opinions, found her own voice. What was so incredibly inspiring about her was that she spoke unapologetically and publicly at a time when women's issues were not seen or thought of as being as important as the issues of men. The unspoken agenda for women at the time was: stand by your man and support his opinions only. Betty wasn't having it. Married to a conservative man, a staid political figure, she had become a true rebel.

Not that she didn't support Gerald. She did, and devotedly. She simply believed her opinions carried equal weight in the sense that she had every right to share them.

I cannot stress how inspirational this message was and is to me. But not just to me. Betty became a hero to women everywhere for her straightforwardness, for being a woman of the times, for demonstrating, in real time, the potential women could reach.

She refused to be defined as a woman of the past. She actively spoke out on the current social issues of her day: Vietnam, abortion rights, women's rights, premarital sex, and marijuana use. It was a radical time, and Betty was no wallflower. She was an outspoken Republican woman who became the voice for all women, no matter their politics. A courageous fighter who for the first time in history openly stated that she had differing opinions than those of her husband—now known as President Gerald Ford. She became a self-realized woman. A woman who moved me to behave as she did. Betty changed the role of First Lady in many ways during a decade that mirrored her change, that demanded change.

At the age of sixteen, she'd watched her mother become a young widow after her father took his life and later discovered her father was an alcoholic, as was her mother. Betty's life changed drastically with these events. She was no stranger to adversity and became a big believer in the importance of honesty and transparency. Both became the foundations by which she lived her life.

Betty rose to the occasion after her husband died—as I did, as all modern widows must—and took steps to be a *helper*. She used her public voice to establish and promote her aims and goals and strategies to make life better for the unempowered, for the underserved, for the voiceless. I have followed her lead. Much like the global widow advocacy happening today, change is being demanded, and like all social/political movements, ours needs a voice and a face to fight the good fight. For us, our brilliant community at Modern Widows Club, that face and voice is me. I couldn't be more honored to lead this charge, couldn't be more proud of the widows who surround me, couldn't be more grateful for Betty's inspirational life-journey.

Betty's bravery in going public about her breast cancer and drug and alcohol addiction saved lives and completely changed the national narrative around these two topics. She spoke personally and painfully of the traumas and struggles in finding a way to recover from these illnesses. Betty's courage should inspire widows to speak up for ourselves when no one understands or shows interest in the challenges of our journey. The public square *must* be made to believe widows when they say they are in distress and need something that doesn't exist for them. That's the fight I'm fighting. The fight all modern widows must continue to fight. Betty Ford inspires me to keep fighting.

Betty's relationship with Gerald warms my heart because this kind of marital equality is what I had too, a true friend-and-champion husband and father to my children. He cherished me like Gerald cherished Betty. A bright light of wisdom that continues to keep me moving forward. To be loved for genuinely who you are, and not what someone else needs you to be for them.

Betty became the national face for drug addiction and recovery, famous for creating the Betty Ford Center. But her real legacy is taking her platform and using it to shine a light on taboo topics that needed to be shared in order to be healed. Widowed for five years at the end of her life, she no doubt missed her husband with all her heart. Throughout their life together, he supported and encouraged her to form her own opinions and to share them with courage and conviction. Their relationship warms my heart and reminds me of my relationship with my late husband.

In her final years, she became fragile and struggled with her health but never with her spirit. She never lost the light of her spirit, as a mother, wife, widow, and compassionate human being. She continues to be a role model for women worldwide. For me.

Betty Ford was a woman whose voice never dimmed—in marriage or in widowhood—whose platform never failed to elevate the honesty, truth, transparency, and vulnerability it took for her to become the grief-to-growth role model into which she evolved. In facing her own brokenness, she shined a light, *her light*, on how important it was—*how important it is*—to find resources for healing and recovery. I will not, I cannot, forget Betty's contribution to my own healing process. I strive to be more like her every day.

QUESTIONS TO CONSIDER

Betty recognized and admitted she had unhealthy coping mechanisms. Have you also realized any unhealthy choices you've made along the way in widowhood?

In what ways have you taken ownership of your widowhood journey?

How do you feel you can create a legacy tribute to your late partner?

ACKNOWLEDGEMENTS

Thank you all the *Wisters* (widow + sisters) at Modern Widows Club and around the world who have filled me with inspiration, strength, love, and light.

Thank you Lyn Kienholz for coordinating our many meetings to develop the book's content.

Thank you J.B. Hunt and Mary Rowin, two very special Modern Widows Club Book Club members who stepped forward and made this book possible, spending months researching and writing each bio.

Thank you Ross Marino, of Luke 12:48 Foundation, and Widow Champion Victor Hurlburt, who saw the need for fueling this project with funding and helped it become the reality it is today. May your investment be a blessing back to you tenfold.

Thank you writer, editor, and book builder Rich Leder, who helped *Stories of Legacy* find focus and guided it through its creative construction. Rich, you championed me through the arc of each biography and Moor Thoughts, ensuring that each piece had a heartbeat that would connect with readers.

Thank you Elaini Caruso for your excellent proofreading skills, which made all the difference in how the stories flowed.

Thank you Michelle Horn for the incredible job of fact checking 12 biographies with your eagle eye.

Thank you Beta Readers for your time and terrific input, especially Laurie Rich, whose clear, sharp take on the book at the very end was invaluable for helping pull all the threads together.

Thank you Morgane Leoni for the fantastic book cover design. So grateful we found one another through Reedsy.com

Believe me when I tell you that teamwork makes the dream work. THANK YOU ALL!

SOURCES

Helen Fabela Chávez

Photo Source: Photo courtesy of TM/© 2023 The Cesar Chavez Foundation

Content Sources: "The Legacy of Helen Chavez," J. Weston Phippen, *Atlantic Magazine*, June 16, 2016; https://ufw.org/helen-fabela-chavez/; "Helen - The Woman Behind the Hero," Jeannette Hernandez, *BeLatina.com*

Terri Irwin

Photo Source: Eva Rinaldi, CC BY-SA 2.0 (creativecommons.org/licenses/by-sa/2.0), via Wikimedia Commons

Content Source: australiazoo.com.au/about-us/the-irwins/; www.thefamouspeople.com/profiles/terri-irwin

Betty White

Photo Source: Alan Light, CC BY 2.0 (creativecommons.org/licenses/by/2.0), via Wikimedia Commons

Content Sources: *Encyclopedia Britannica;* Biography.com; Wikipedia.org.; "Women Who Shaped History, A *Smithsonian Magazine* Special Report," January 22, 2022.

Cindy McCain

Photo Source: United States Department of State, Public domain, via Wikimedia Commons

Content Sources: *Encyclopedia Britannica;* McCain Institute; Politico.com; *Stronger: Courage, Hope, and Humor in My Life with John McCain* by Cindy McCain

Katharine Meyer Graham

Photo Source: Anefo, CC0 via Wikimedia Commons

Content Source: *Personal History* by Katharine Graham

Coretta Scott King

Photo Source: John Mathew Smith & www.celebrity-photos.com, CC BY-SA 2.0 (creativecommons.org/licenses/by-sa/2.0), via Wikimedia Commons

Content Sources: *Coretta Scott King and the Center for Nonviolent Social Change*, Jackie F. Stanmyre; Thekingcenter.org; *Encyclopedia Britannica*

Graça Machel

Photo Source: Fronteiras do Pensamento, CC BY-SA 2.0 (creativecommons.org/licenses/by-sa/2.0), via Wikimedia Commons

Content Sources: http://www.nytimes.com/1996/03/20/world/south-african-judge-gives-nelson-mandela-a-divorce.html; http://www.npr.org/blogs/parallels/2013/06/11/190671704/the-day-nelson-mandela-walked-out-of-prison; http://www.nytimes.com/1998/02/19/world/johannesburg-journal-of-leaders-and-lovers-a-south-african-epidemic.html; https://www.quotes.net/citizen-quote/24814

Te Ata Thompson Fisher

Photo Source: Courtesy of Chickasaw Nation

Content Sources: *The Encyclopedia of Oklahoma History and Culture*; Chickasaw Hall of Fame; *Te Ata: Chickasaw Storyteller, American Treasure* by Richard Green

Osa Johnson

Photo Source: George Eastman House, Public domain via Wikimedia Commons

Content Sources: Encyclopedia Britannica; *I Married Adventure: The Lives of Martin and Osa Johnson* by Osa Johnson; https://freerangeamerican.us/martin-and-osa-johnson/

Veuve Clicquot

Photo Source: Léon Cogniet, Public domain, via Wikimedia Commons

Content Source: *The Widow Clicquot* by Tilar J. Mazzeo

Eleanor Roosevelt

Photo Source: National Archives and Records Administration, Public domain, via Wikimedia Commons

Content Sources: "Eleanor Roosevelt's Remarkable Transition from the White House into Widowhood, 1945-1946," article by Harold Smith, published in *Illness, Crisis and Loss*, Sage Journals, 2017; The National First Ladies Library website: www.firstladies.org/biographies

Betty Ford

Photo Source: David Hume Kennerly, Public domain, via Wikimedia Commons

Content Sources: *Encyclopedia Britannica;* The Gerald R. Ford Presidential Library and Museum

Made in the USA
Monee, IL
24 August 2023